Efficient E-Procurement with SAP®

SAP® Essentials

Expert SAP knowledge for your day-to-day work

Whether you wish to expand your SAP knowledge, deepen it, or master a use case, SAP Essentials provide you with targeted expert knowledge that helps support you in your day-to-day work. To the point, detailed, and ready to use.

SAP PRESS is a joint initiative of SAP and Galileo Press. The know-how offered by SAP specialists combined with the expertise of the Galileo Press publishing house offers the reader expert books in the field. SAP PRESS features first-hand information and expert advice, and provides useful skills for professional decision-making.

SAP PRESS offers a variety of books on technical and business related topics for the SAP user. For further information, please visit our website: *www.sap-press.com.*

Marc Hoppe
Inventory Optimization with SAP
2008, 705 pp.
978-1-59229-205-9

Martin Murray
SAP MM-Functionality and Technical Configuration (Second Edition)
2008, 588 pp.
978-1-59229-134-2

Padma Prasad Munirathinam and Ramakrishna Potluri
Consultant's Guide to SAP SRM
2008, 512 pp.
978-1-59229-154-0

Eduard Gerhardt, Kai Krüger, Oliver Schipp

Efficient E-Procurement with SAP®

Galileo Press

Bonn • Boston

Contents

1 Introduction

Procurement processing is defined by numerous codified regulations in both the public and private sectors. For example, compliance requirements in the private sector — that is, complying with the rules of conduct and guidelines of procurement —assume the role of complex order placement regulations in the public sector. Moreover, operational procurement processing is characterized by complex communication and reconciliation processes, from determining requirements, to submitting legally binding orders, to posting goods receipts.

Regulations in procurement

SAP offers a wide range of tools for procurement processing. That means that all processes are supported, from value-based procurement documentation (in the form of vendor invoices in Financial Accounting), to complex logistical processing in the Materials Management (MM) component (SAP ERP), to e-procurement (SAP SRM).

Procurement with SAP

However, selecting the appropriate tool is very difficult and depends on the existing organizational structure, and the type and frequency of the procurement process. The goal of this book is to describe the factors that influence the decision, configuration, and use of the respective SAP tool for procurement processing. It focuses on e-procurement in SAP SRM.

Selecting the procurement tool

1.1 Structure of the Book

Chapter 2, Basic Principles of Procurement, outlines the initial situation and related general issues in conjunction with the selection of the appropriate procurement procedure.

Chapter 3, Factors that Influence the Procurement Organization, discusses the legal basis, in particular current compliance requirements and order placement regulations, in the public sector. It then covers the procurement organization. This information focuses on how the organization and legal form affects procurement processing and the centralization and decentralization of procurement tasks. The heterogeneity of the involved organizational units has no direct influence on the scope of the procurement range. The chapter closes with details on how procurement intensity affects the selection of the appropriate purchasing tools.

The tools available for automatic procurement processing are introduced in **Chapter 4,** Implementing Procurement Processing in SAP ERP. The chapter first describes the prerequisites for procurement processing within Financial Accounting, without the involvement of logistics. It then compares the prerequisites for procurement processing with logistics in the SAP component *MM* and procurement processing via e-procurement. The comparison focuses on the disadvantages, advantages, and limits of these usage scenarios.

Based on this, **Chapter 5**, Implementing Procurement Processing in SAP SRM, explains the implementation of procurement-related tasks within *SAP Supplier Relationship Management* (SAP SRM). In this context, the chapter also provides details on the central component, that is, the integrated goods catalog (which is similar to the material master records in MM). The solution's integration capability for supporting procurement processing is described from both internal and external viewpoints.

Chapter 6, Reporting for Procurement Controlling, discusses the reporting functions for procurement controlling, which consist of standard and individual reports. The topics of complaints processing and possible escalations complete the description of the procurement process. The included figures illustrate the process flow with all involved roles and tasks. **Chapter 7**, Summary and Outlook, compares the procedures that were introduced, including their advantages and disadvantages, in the context of specific usage scenarios.

The **Appendix** contains key transactions, categorized by business objects within the Accounts Payable Accounting and MM components of SAP ERP. It also provides an overview of the purchasing processes.

1.2 Target Audience

Target groups This book is intended for all persons responsible in the materials management or purchasing departments of commercial and administrative enterprises. Recommended actions can be derived for both the operational and the strategic orientation of procurement activities. This book contains approaches for the improvement of processes and differentiates by the type and quality of the material to be procured.

Readers should have sound business knowledge of materials management and logistics. They should also be familiar with the SAP components MM and Financial Accounting (FI).

Prerequisites for reading the book

2   Basic Principles of Procurement

In general terms, *procurement* is comprised of all of the activities necessary to provide an enterprise with the goods necessary to support its
business activities. The types of activities and the required knowledge
depend heavily on the complexity and type of the commodities and services to be procured.

What is
procurement?

The activities required for this are called the *procurement process*, which
refers to the operational procurement processing and all activities that pre-
cede the order process (including market analyses and vendor selection, as well as downstream activities, such as goods receipt or quality
inspection). To optimize procurement with electronic tools, you must
take a look at the entire procurement process, from the determination
of requirements to the ongoing supply of materials. The type of procurement process is defined by the type of goods (commodities and services)
to be procured. You must achieve a balance between the effort associated
with an order and the resulting business benefit.

In general, procurement can be divided into *strategic procurement management* and *operational purchasing*.

The main task of strategic procurement management is the central –
or cross-organizational – coordination of goods and services procurement. This includes various individual activities, such as requirements
grouping, classifying and selecting the procurement market, managing
relationships with vendors, and performing material-related value and
quality analyses. The supply quality therefore directly affects customer
satisfaction or market acceptance of the enterprise.

Strategic
procurement
management

The main task of operational purchasing is actual procurement. Its key
function is to supply the enterprise with materials at the lowest possible
cost in terms of time, quality, quantity, and space. This is achieved by
checking incoming procurement requests, entering resulting orders in
an information system, and posting goods and invoice receipts. Other

Operational
purchasing

critical activities of operational purchasing include stock-keeping and warehouse management, including inventory management.

Procurement controlling

As a business control and coordination instrument, comprehensive procurement controlling should ensure transparency across the strategic and operational procurement processes (see Figure 2.1). Therefore, particular attention is paid to the strategic relevance of purchasing and material logistics.

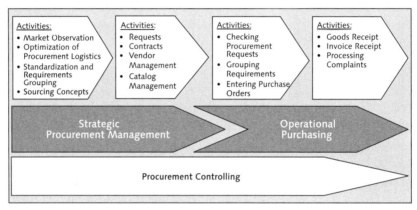

Figure 2.1 Procurement Processes

Enterprise-internal procurement processes are determined primarily through technical specificity (that is, the special characteristics of the goods to be procured that can only be used for specific purposes due to their physical nature), existing organizational structure, and software support.

What is procured?

The impact of technical specificity on the procurement workflow becomes obvious when you compare the procurement of complex measuring devices with the procurement of common office supplies. There are significant differences concerning the process flow, from determining and specifying requirements, to vendor selection, to processing the ongoing supply. The technical variety of possible procurement transactions clearly shows that to optimize the process with electronic tools and select the appropriate tool, the entire procurement process has to be considered.

The organizational structure in materials management (central, decentralized, partially centralized, or other), the legal form (private or public), and the size of the organization also affect the enterprise-internal procurement workflow. In centrally and decentrally organized purchasing processes, for example, considerable differences exist with regard to how requirements are determined and procurement requests are forwarded.

Organizational structure

The software also indirectly defines the process flow and organizational structure via the scope of the functions provided (for example, to enter procurement requests, and approve and group them). If the software doesn't let you group requirements automatically, you'll have to use workarounds to compensate. This again affects the process and organizational structure. Therefore, optimizing procurement processes, general processes, organizational structures, and roles always requires new software and, depending on the type of the goods to be procured, has to be coordinated with the various systems and persons responsible.

In commercial and administrative enterprises, three fundamentally different procurement departments involved in the procurement processes typically exist:

Procurement departments

▶ HR department: responsible for procuring labor

▶ Capital department: responsible for procuring capital

▶ Purchasing department: responsible for procuring materials, trade goods, services, capital equipment, and information

Processes related to the procurement of human resources and capital are excluded from our discussion, and we only make reference to the supporting SAP products *Human Capital* Management (HCM) and *Treasury* (TR).

This book focuses on the processes in the purchasing department. The term "purchasing department" is rather unspecific and very flexible. It is therefore often used to refer exclusively to processes employed in materials management. A strong focus on materials management leads to ignoring critical parts of those procurement items whose individual steps (such as the purchase order or goods receipt) don't have to be mapped in detail within the supply chain. Consequently, a significant portion of procurement items is not adequately supported by software, such as the

Processes in the Purchasing department

procurement of office supplies, ad-hoc purchases of low-value goods or material, or services that don't directly add value. Because these processes sometimes involve payment flows before an order can be entered in the system, the activities are only mapped in the financial management system.

For some enterprises, particularly in the service and public sectors, procurement items with non-essential logistical processes, such as delivery and storage, comprise a main part of purchasing. To be able to define the corresponding software support within the SAP world, this book therefore describes all output-relevant processes in an enterprise (excluding the procurement of human resources and capital) that are related to the receipt and processing of invoices issued by vendors or to incoming invoices.

3 Factors that Influence the Procurement Organization

The procurement range and frequency significantly influence an enterprise's procurement organization. Depending on the heterogeneity of requirements, organization structures and communication paths must be set up within an enterprise to enable purchasing to implement the required procurement items productively, quickly, cost-efficiently, and according to compliance standards. This presupposes that the capabilities provided in the SAP systems are optimally used in the contexts of procurement range and procurement intensity.

3.1 Procurement Range

The *procurement range* – that is, the range of all possible procurement processes – has a strong influence on the organization of procurement.

As the complexity of the goods to be processed increases, the communication relationships between operational purchasing and strategic purchasing also become more complicated and extensive.

You can remove this complexity from the organizational structure and simplify the entire process flow by standardizing material groups within the enterprise. Material groups enable you to classify and structure the entire range of goods on offer – both horizontally and vertically (see Figure 3.1) – and throughout the enterprise, each item is uniquely assigned to a material group.

Material groups

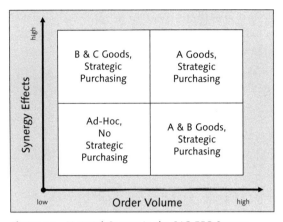

Figure 3.1 Material Groups in the SAP ERP System

ABC analysis A common organization procedure to classify a large number of objects or materials is the *ABC analysis*, which attempts to make a distinction between essential and nonessential materials. It is a useful tool for preparing streamlining measures and to channel work activities in materials management. The following classification enables you to reduce economically non-effective efforts through simplification measures.

In materials management, the ABC analysis is used, for example, to examine one or more of the following:

▸ Number and value of the consumed/procured material groups or material items

▸ Number and value of all purchase orders

▸ Number and value of vendor invoices

▸ Number and value of complaints

▸ Business volume value per vendor

Classification of Targeted channeling of the processing effort in materials management
materials attempts to distinguish between essential and nonessential data or objects.

In addition to quantity- and value-based values, the ABC analysis assumes that the standardization potential and the resulting synergy effects increase continuously from A materials to C materials (as seen in Table 3.1).

Material type		Value limits	Quantities
A material	Low quantity-based percentage; high value-based percentage	60 – 80%	15 – 25%
B material	Average quantity-based percentage; low value-based percentage	10 – 25%	30 – 40%
C material	High quantity-based percentage; low value-based percentage	5 – 15%	40 – 70%

Table 3.1 Classification of the ABC Analysis

3.1.1 A Materials

If you want to have large, cost-saving purchasing volumes, you should first consider *A materials* because these are the most valuable and have the highest cost-saving potential.

Frequently, the cost of keeping these procurement goods in stock is significant. In this context, managing goods in a way that avoids stock and precisely determines low safety stock levels is highly critical. Central purchasing should be responsible for exact requirements planning of quantities and dates. Program-controlled *requirements determination* in combination with precise inventory management results in short delivery intervals and additional cost-savings.

Stockholding costs

Using multiple information sources, you should establish a system of continuous market research and pricing analysis for A items. The enterprise should also have alternative vendors to ensure production and service levels. Purchase order handling is characterized by thorough preparation and implementation. This entails strict deadline control, exact invoice verification, and precise quantity and quality checks.

Market research and pricing analysis

3.1.2 C Materials

Usually, *C items* are characterized by a relatively low single value with a comparably frequent ordering interval, and high ordering effort and delivery volume.

High costs caused by high volumes

In principle, these are standardized products that create relatively high costs resulting from accumulated procurement volumes. Possible causes of these high costs include the following:

▸ Multifaceted, complex procurement processes

▸ Centrally organized and formally controlled procurement

▸ Ordering processes that take longer than delivery

▸ Large number of vendors and high percentage of small purchase orders as a result of minor price advantages and short-term requirements

Effort for the Purchasing department

Moreover, C materials bind (human) resources in purchasing departments, which then can't be used for other tasks, such as procuring A materials. Accordingly, provisioning or management of goods should be stock-related and not requirement-related. All process-related costs should be kept low through simple material requirements planning procedures without considering stock. You can simplify purchase order handling by not implementing any deadline control, invoice verification, or quality checks.

Therefore, C item management requires a holistic optimization of processes, tools and procurement strategies. The goal of such approaches is to decrease process costs, reduce lead times, facilitate procurement processes, achieve favorable purchase prices (thanks to requirements grouping), and ensure the availability and quality of the goods.

3.1.3   ABC Analyses

Total consumption

ABC analyses examine the quantity-based and value-based total consumption within a specific period, based on statistical analysis. In the long run, however, the flow of consumption of individual materials over a longer period of time is also important. Within the planning period, the quantity consumed of some goods is relatively constant, while the quantity consumed of other goods is irregular or subject to fluctuations. Against this background, you can classify materials according to the forecast accuracy of their consumption (see Table 3.2).

Category	Consumption	Forecast accuracy
X goods	Constant, with rare or only minor fluctuations	High
Y goods	Stronger fluctuations due to trends or seasonal influences	Medium
Z goods	Extremely irregular or random	Low

Table 3.2 Forecast Accuracy for Procurement Objects

Compared to the ABC analysis, the forecast accuracy analysis is subject to a method that can't be calculated directly, and is therefore – at least partly – subjective.

By combining the ABC and XYZ analyses you can determine the matrix shown in Table 3.3, which you can use to derive consequences for the requirements planning of the corresponding goods.

XYZ analysis

Classification/ Forecast accuracy	A	B	C
X	High consumption value High forecast accuracy	Average consumption value High forecast accuracy	Low consumption value High forecast accuracy
Y	High consumption value Average forecast accuracy	Average consumption value Average forecast accuracy	Low consumption value Average forecast accuracy
Z	High consumption value Low forecast accuracy	Average consumption value Low forecast accuracy	Low consumption value Low forecast accuracy

Table 3.3 Combining ABC and XYZ Analyses

Because of their particular relevance, we will recommend actions for processing AX and BY goods.

AX parts   Requirements planning for AX parts follows a deterministic requirements calculation, to arrive at exact delivery times and quantities. To select suppliers, it is particularly important to consider comparison factors such as reliability, flexibility, or integration capability. Contracts with strategic partners should be designed for the long term and provide a procurement path directly from the manufacturer.

BY parts   For BY parts, however, you must take into consideration that the requirements calculation can be stochastic, and that order quantities should be oriented towards optimal lot sizes to facilitate the entire process. For selecting vendors, comparison factors such as the cost price, delivery service, and synergy effects are relevant.

3.2   Procurement Organization

The procurement organization should efficiently and effectively coordinate the flow of all strategic and operational activities that are required to supply an enterprise with goods.

Central and decentralized activities   Often, the challenge is to harmonize decentralized operational activities with centralized strategic tasks, without loss of information. This requires technical utilities and balanced task distribution between strategic and operational purchasing to limit the immanent loss of information, communication effort, and procurement lead times.

In central operational purchasing with decentralized origin of requirements, you can, for example, reduce procurement process costs via concentrated process knowledge only if the communication flow between requisitioner and purchaser is efficient and effective. If disrupting factors are present, you won't be able to meet commitments because of incorrect or delayed deliveries, or because of time-intensive communication.

3.2.1   Strategic Procurement Management

The main task of strategic procurement management is to lay a suitable foundation for achieving the goals of modern procurement, for example, the reduction of purchase and process costs.

Procurement management is responsible for cross-organizational standardization of the item and service portfolio to utilize synergy effects, and to decrease follow-up and maintenance costs. The strategic specifications constitute the framework of operational purchasing.

Procurement management

The first task of strategic procurement management is the central or corporate-wide coordination of goods and services procurement, which, in turn, results in many individual activities such as requirements grouping, implementation of awards of contracts or bids, and conclusion of outline agreements.

Coordination

Because the main goal of classic strategic purchasing is to decrease purchase prices and keep follow-up and maintenance costs as low as possible, you should centrally procure those goods and services that have a high order volume or let you use synergy effects. A high order volume, for example, results in improved purchasing conditions. The use of synergy effects through the central integration of specific expertise and bundling multiple procurement processes results in reduced process costs. You can minimize follow-up and maintenance costs through adherence to standards and homogenization of the items to be procured.

Reducing the purchase prices

The savings potentials can only be attained, however, if the order data is continuously evaluated throughout the enterprise within procurement controlling, and if you quickly respond to trends emerging from the order data by negotiating new outline agreements or modifying existing agreements. Table 3.4 outlines the main tasks of a strategic purchaser.

Tasks of the strategic purchaser

The tasks of a strategic procurement manager – usually comprehensive in nature – require the centralization of strategic procurement management. For example, all procurement processes with high order volume, and goods with high synergy effects, must be purchased strategically. A high order volume is usually only possible if requirements are bundled across the organization. You can ensure the use of synergy effects in procurement and in downstream usage only if standards are determined for specific goods. By standardizing item portfolios you can also reduce follow-up and maintenance costs.

Tasks of the strategic purchaser

Task	Description	Procedure
Systematic market survey	Check possible new goods; search for innovations	No system reference
Standardization and requirements grouping		No system reference, evaluations in the SAP ERP system
Consulting	Consulting requisitioners with regard to goods and services to be procured, for example, with regard to standardization and unification	No system reference
Implementing competitions/ tenders		E-award system/no system reference
Implementing awards of contracts		E-award system
Managing SAP master data	Initiating the creation of master data and monitoring of its up-to-dateness (vendor and material master data); outline agreements in the SAP system	SAP ERP system
Catalog management	Managing e-catalog maintenance	SAP SRM system
Information manager	Actively notifying operational purchasing about innovations and changes; assistance with the assignment to Materials Management (MM) goods and service groups	No system reference/ SAP ERP system/ SAP SRM system
Complaint handling	Complaint handling at the vendor in case of escalation	No system reference
Strategic controlling	Monitoring outline agreements; monitoring the vendor base; evaluating orders for further procurement optimization	SAP ERP system, SAP SRM system

Table 3.4 Tasks of a Strategic Purchaser

Enterprises frequently try to implement a value-oriented participation obligation of the strategic procurement manager (e.g., the procurement value is higher than $2,500 net). This value-oriented contribution limit is not compatible with the requirements of strategic purchasing and does not fit into current day procurement practices. Practical experience has shown that a value-oriented contribution limit can easily be bypassed by distributing procurement to multiple orders. The necessity of strategic purchasing results from not only high order volumes, but also from possible synergy effects, which can also be reached through low order volumes. Therefore, you should replace any price-oriented participation obligation with a participation obligation that complies with goods and service classifications.

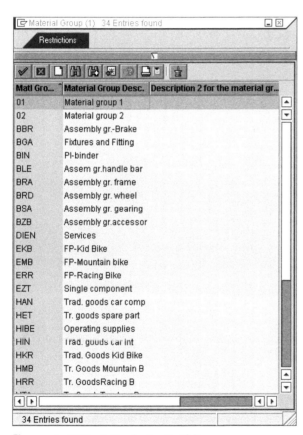

Figure 3.2 Strategic Purchasing Portfolio

Excursion: Centralization of Strategic Procurement Management

In the public sector, the demand for the centralization of strategic procurement management is further increased by the requirement to obtain bids for goods that are subject to strategic purchasing. Strategic procurement managers should therefore have sole bid and award of contract authority to efficiently and correctly handle bids. Consequently, commissioning award of contract know-how at a decentralized level is not required.

E-award platform

Another reason for the centralization of strategic procurement management is the introduction of an e-award platform in the public sector. This platform is used to handle the entire award of contract process electronically, and with Internet support. Here, the accumulating award of contract requirements should be bundled by only a few central jobs and handled in the e-award system.

3.2.2 Operational Purchasing

The operational purchaser deals with short-term decisions in daily business. Activities of operational purchasing include the system-based implementation of procurement (in the SAP ERP or the SAP SRM), checking procurement requests, entering orders into the system, and posting goods and invoice receipts.

Persons involved in operational purchasing

Compared to strategic purchasing, the operational purchasing organization is considerably more complex, because many different parties are involved and because the enterprise's organization itself exerts direct influence. The organizational structure of operational purchasing includes the following basic roles:

- Requester
- Approver
- Operational purchaser

The heterogeneity of tasks, resulting from the implementation of these roles, causes a wide circle of persons to be involved within the enterprise. This poses great challenges for the functions of the systems used for handling procurement processes.

Requester

Any employee can be a requester because the need for consumption goods (indirect/MRO items) can emerge in any area of the enterprise.

To avoid loss of information and to ensure that the required goods necessary to carry out tasks correspond as much as possible to the goods actually provided, requisitioners should directly notify or describe the procurement request. For this purpose they can:

Procurement requests

▶ Complete a purchase requisition form

▶ Enter the purchase requisition in the SAP ERP system

▶ Compile a shopping cart in the SAP SRM system (see Chapter 5, Implementing Procurement Processing in SAP SRM)

Before requirement notifications can be converted into legally binding orders by purchasers, they must be approved by approvers in compliance with defined approval rules.

Approver

The principle of the separation of functions necessitates that an order can only be triggered based on an approved purchase requisition. The task of an approver is to approve in compliance with defined approval rules and based on principles and values.

Operational Purchaser

The role of operational purchaser includes the authority of system-supported handling of procurement processes and legally binding conclusion of contracts. Table 3.5 contains a detailed description of the range of tasks.

Task	Description	Procedure
Interface function	Interface to the strategic procurement manager	No system reference
Requirements grouping	Grouping of requirements and, if necessary, forwarding to strategic procurement management	No system reference
Consulting	Consulting requisitioners with regard to goods and services to be procured	No system reference
Master data management	Maintaining master data in the SAP system at the plant level (vendor and material master data)	SAP ERP system
Order entry	Entering orders and submitting orders to vendors	SAP ERP system
Goods receipt	Posting of goods receipt according to the dual-control principle (see Section 5.5 on compliance with the dual-control principle). For inventory-managed materials, goods receipt can be posted by the warehouse clerk	SAP ERP system, SAP SRM system
Invoice receipt	Content and amount verification, as well as entry of vendor invoices according to the dual-control principle	SAP ERP system, SAP SRM system
Complaints	Complaint processing at the vendor, informing the strategic purchaser in case of escalation	No system reference
Operational controlling	Order history, vendor evaluation, etc.	SAP ERP system, SAP SRM system

Table 3.5 Tasks of the Operational Purchaser

Role of the operational purchaser

You can derive the following central requirements of the operational purchaser's role from his tasks:

- Negotiation skills and knowledge of contract design, at least for requirements that are not subject to strategic purchasing

- Market and technical knowledge of the material groups to be procured

- Process knowledge with regard to system-supported handling of procurement processes in the SAP ERP system and/or SAP SRM system

As these requirements show, the operational purchaser's role can't be assumed by a person with only sporadic purchasing activities. Rather, these requirements can be fulfilled effectively only if the role of the operational purchaser is assumed by a qualified full-time employee who has the appropriate purchasing, product and system expertise.

In an enterprise whose organization is highly decentralized and that has geographically distributed subsidiaries, you can define the organizational location of the operational purchaser only after an in-depth analysis of the requirement range and the procurement volume.

This will be illustrated based on an example. The sample enterprise shown in Figure 3.3 is characterized by a head office with many geographically distributed subsidiaries (SUB) that have different procurement volumes and a heterogeneous consumption of material groups. The size of the circles represents the scope of the order volume, and the shade of the circles reflect the heterogeneous requirements.

Example

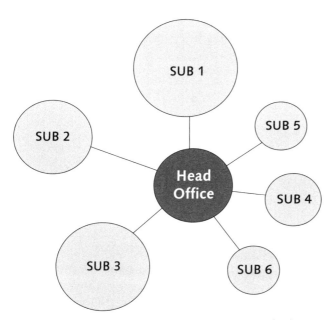

Figure 3.3 Decentrally Organized Enterprise (SUB = Subsidiary)

For economic reasons, the order volumes of subsidiaries 4, 5, and 6 don't allow for an operational purchaser (i.e., the familiarization effort for the system-supported procurement processing as well as the setup times are too high compared to the low task volume). Subsidiaries 1, 2, and 3, however, can be the base for operational purchasing because of

their high procurement intensity. Moreover, in addition to the standard requirements, they have
 subsidiary-specific goods in their consumption portfolio. The procurement of complex measuring devices at subsidiary 3 and the procurement of various road signs at subsidiaries 1 and 2 account for a major portion of the overall purchase activities.

A suitable procurement organization in this decentrally organized enterprise would be to handle the procurement for subsidiaries 4, 5, and 6 through the operational purchasers of subsidiaries 1 and 3. A smooth supply of standard goods for these subsidiaries requires forwarding of requirement specifications to the operational purchaser applying little effort and great precision. Because of their special requirements, subsidiaries 1, 2, and 3 require additional procurement know-how related to their requirement range. As a result of the similar consumption at subsidiaries 1 and 2 it makes economic sense to concentrate the purchasing of special goods (road signs) at subsidiary 1.

Bundling purchasing activities at a few locations in the enterprise enables an aggregation of task volume. Consequently, the prerequisites are met to employ persons whose primary responsibility is purchasing and who don't have to assume additional tasks (as is often the case for service providing organizations).

The following sections describe the possible locations for the operational purchaser. Where this person will ultimately be located within the enterprise can only be decided on a case-by-case basis.

Complete Centralization

Combined in one department

For complete centralization, all operational purchasing within an enterprise is combined into one department. Consequently, the enterprise's entire range of requirements can be procured only by the professional purchasers in that department. In individual departments, employees can be assigned with procurement tasks based on the e-procurement system. However, you must consider that the centralization of purchasing authority involves relocation or assignment of competencies. For enterprises with a strongly decentralized organization, this organizational structure may encounter strong resistance.

Outsourcing

Another option – for example, for locations with low procurement volumes – is to completely transfer operational procurement activities to a central service provider. At the individual subsidiaries, employees can be assigned procurement tasks based on the e-procurement system.

External service providers

Organization-Oriented Partial Centralization

The goal of organization-oriented partial centralization is to bundle an enterprise's operational purchasing responsibility in purchasing departments that are responsible for multiple subsidiaries. The bundling of purchasing authority can be implemented by either considering regional aspects or the requirement range. In the individual administrative offices, employees can be assigned with procurement tasks based on the e-procurement system.

Enterprises with many subsidiaries

This organizational structure is particularly suitable for enterprises with many geographically distributed subsidiaries. By creating regional procurement centers you can, on the one hand, establish physical proximity to requisitioners and, on the other hand, minimize potential organizational resistance to relocation or assignment of competencies.

Material Group-Oriented Partial Centralization

For material group-oriented partial centralization procurement authority is bundled for selected material groups, in one or more procurement departments at the enterprise level. The procurement responsibility for the remaining material groups stays with the administrative offices.

This enables you to, for example, centrally procure complex goods, such as PCs or vehicles, for which you require special procurement know-how. Less complex convenience goods, such as office supplies, books, and so on, can be purchased decentralized by the administrative offices. For this purpose, employees at the individual subsidiaries are assigned with procurement tasks based on the e-procurement system.

Separation by special goods

The material group-oriented partial centralization is a very flexible procurement organizational structure and is widely used. By bundling the material group-specific know-how at one location, the cost-effective, decentralized provision of know-how and the laborious individual familiarization of the purchaser with the specifics of complex goods become obsolete. Simultaneously, you can ensure technically correct and cost-efficient procurement for complex goods.

3.3 Corporate Governance

The term *corporate governance* (CG) is the legal and factual framework for responsible management and monitoring, oriented towards long-term added value. Recently, corporate governance has again gained in importance and directly influences the organization and documentation of business transactions within an enterprise.

According to the Compliance Institute, enterprises must take into consideration more than 100 regulations and laws globally. Moreover, management is obliged to provide revision-proof evidence for their business transactions.

IT governance   You can directly derive requirements or consequences for IT governance from corporate governance. The goal is to control and monitor the use of IT enterprises in such a way that you can achieve a controlled and efficient use of IT.

To ensure compliance – that is, to fulfill legal and factual requirements – you must use an internal control system to monitor the following components:

- Flow of IT-based business processes
- Application systems
- IT infrastructure

To derive the necessary controls you must observe numerous codified and non-codified rule sets, for example:

Compliance rule sets
- German Control and Transparency in Business Act (KonTraG)
- German Corporate Governance Codex (DCGK)
- Sarbanes-Oxley Act (SOX)

- Principles of proper accounting and balancing
- Principles of proper IT-based accounting systems

All of these rules have in common that the transaction flow of information is recorded within the framework of process handling from initiation to disclosure, including revision-proof documentation to identify violations or errors. To control risks in business processes, they must be identified and documented in advance. Consequently, all business processes, along with their underlying application systems and infrastructure components, must be continuously recorded in the documentation. Based on the documentation, you can then establish process-immanent security measures, such as workflows, downstream controls, and so on.

Procurement is a fundamental business process and forms the basis for most payment transactions within an enterprise. Because of its importance and its direct public obviousness (shareholders, stakeholders, and the general public), adherence to compliance is particularly critical and has a direct influence on how procurement processes are handled. Therefore, when you decide on the type of process handling in materials management, in the Financial Accounting component of the SAP ERP system, or in the SAP SRM system, you must give priority to the process variant that ensures comprehensive, revision-proof documentation and thus considerably reduces the risk of misuse. This requirement is enforced by the Sabames Oxley Act, which states that management is obligated to establish a monitoring system in the enterprise for early detection or prevention of perilous developments.

Compliance in procurement

4 Implementing Procurement Processing in SAP ERP

In the SAP ERP system, procurement can be processed in different ways using the following basic options: procurement without logistical processing – Financial Accounting (FI) – or procurement with logistical processing – Materials Management (MM).

The following sections describe the different procurement types as well as the two mentioned options for procurement processing.

4.1 The Different Procurement Types

A wide range of output-relevant procurement processes exist. In the Business Process Repository (BPR) of SAP Solution Manager, for example, SAP distinguishes between PROCUREMENT WITH LOGISTIC and PROCUREMENT WITHOUT LOGISTIC (see Figure 4.1). The process steps highlighted in bold in the Figure (within the processes) are mandatory for the processes. All other process steps are optional.

```
Procurement with Logistic [47X200]
        Create purchase requisition
        Create purchase requisition for commitment
        Derive FM account assignment
        Create purchase order
        Post open invoice
        Post funds commitment
        Pay open invoice

Procurement without Logistic [47X200]
        Create funds reservation
        Update funds reservation
        Create funds precommitment
        Change status of funds reservation or precommitment
        Create funds commitment
        Reassign funds commitment
        Adjust funds commitment
        Reduce funds commitment manually
        Change status funds commitment/ invoice
        Post open invoice
        Post funds commitment
        Pay open invoice
```

Figure 4.1 Procurement Process in the BPR of SAP Solution Manager (BPR in SAP Solution Manager)

Procurement without logistic is highly significant in day-to-day business. For the average SAP client, these processes represent approximately 40% of all procurement transactions (see Table 4.1).

Process key figures	Number	Ratio
Cleared vendor invoice in Financial Accounting (FI)	3,680	39%
Cleared vendor invoice in Materials Management (MM)	5,695	61%

Table 4.1 MM Ratio; 3 Month Average, Based on a Sample of 400 SAP Clients

These values have been determined by IBIS Prof. Thome AG in the context of retrograde analyses of live SAP systems. They are based on the analyses of more than 400 SAP operational clients, and the assumption that most procurement processes without logistic in the SAP system are processed via the Financial accounting (FI) component. The ratio of 40% indicates that you shouldn't leave the processing of these processes to chance. Rather, you need to define detailed internal specifications and guidelines to ensure a compliant implementation.

These two procurement categories have the same effect on the posting procedures in Financial Accounting (FI). In the accounts payable ledger, they both generate payables that affect payment. However, all upstream processes are different. For example, procurement with logistic starts in Materials Management, with a purchase requisition or purchase order that is forwarded to Financial Accounting (FI) when the received invoice is entered. This involves detailed documentation of the procurement transaction with regard to type, quality, quantity, and so on.

Procurement without logistic starts with posting a vendor invoice and generating an open item in the SAP system. All upstream processes, such as technical invoice verification, are processed outside the system. Furthermore, the process is documented only in general ledger (G/L) accounts based on values. These differences clearly show that different tools are needed to efficiently support the various processes.

4.2   Procurement Without Logistical Processing

System-supported procurement without logistic can be limited to the process of entering incoming invoices into G/L accounts. You can start this process variant either in the Financial Accounting (FI) or MM component because both components provide entry functions for vendor invoices. Thus, in the SAP system, support of the procurement process without logistic begins when the incoming invoice is entered. All upstream processes, such as procurement requests, request processes, or orders, are processed outside the SAP system or are not required at all.

The following sections describe two options of procurement in the SAP system without logistical processing.

4.2.1   Entering Vendor Invoices in Financial Accounting (FI)

You use Transaction FB60 (Enter Incoming Invoices) to enter vendor invoices. By posting vendor invoices directly to Financial Accounting (FI), procurements without logistic are documented in a technical and value-based manner. In the technical documentation, the process is assigned to an expense or balance sheet account.

Technical documentation

In the value-based documentation, the invoiced amounts are assigned to the relevant G/L accounts and cost centers. The logistical documentation is rather basic because the quantities procured and units of measure are entered on each G/L account (see Figure 4.2). However, these specifications are documented only for information but not controlling purposes.

Value-based documentation

If, for example, the procurement of four high-quality ball pens at a price of $100.00 each is directly processed in the Financial Accounting (FI) component without logistic in the SAP system, the transaction is posted to a subledger account, for example, JOHN NASH LLC (number 1125), with the value of $400.00, and to a G/L account, for example, Office Supplies, (account number 405200) with the same value. In addition, the quantity of 4 can also be entered as the base unit of measure, which is PC (pieces) in this example. By default, no plausibility checks can be performed for quantity specifications and base units of measure. For example, the combination of 4 in the QUANTITY field and PC in the BASE

Example

UNIT OF MEASURE field may be formally correct, but is incorrect with regard to the content. Without plausibility checks, logistically incorrect documentation of procurement transactions can result, which in turn impairs procurement controlling results. The information system would identify "4 hours ball pens," for example.

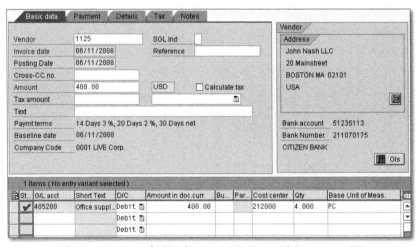

Figure 4.2 Data Entry View of a Vendor Invoice in Financial Accounting (FI)

Validation This disadvantage of logistical documentation can be eliminated using validation in accounting documents. Here, values are checked for permitted value combinations when they are entered in the entry fields so that only permitted data is entered. This way you can use the system to ensure that only PC (pieces) can be entered in the BASE UNIT OF MEASURE field for postings to the G/L account 405200 OFFICE SUPPLIES (see Figure 4.3).

However, the options of individually created validation algorithms are limited because the verification can only be performed on the basis of the G/L account. You can post different procurement transactions, and consequently different base units of measure, to a G/L account such as office supplies. For example, you can post services measured in hours and stationery measured in pieces. In practice, vendor invoices are not logistically documented when they are entered directly in the Financial Accounting (FI) component because the error rate is too high and the ability to evaluate the results is low.

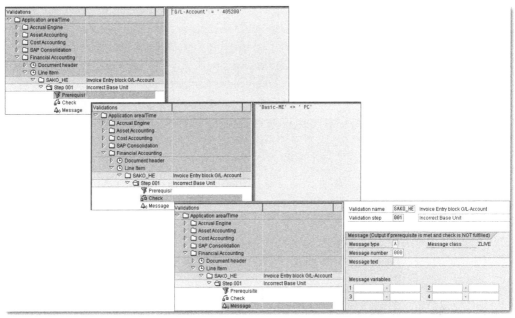

Figure 4.3 Customizing the Validation

The result of the process described previously is a posting record in the form of an "expense account to vendor" (see Figure 4.4). The posting key (PK) 40 in the second item of the document represents the debit posting to a G/L account (an expense account in this example), and the posting key (PK) 31 in the first line item represents a credit posting to a subledger account (a vendor in this example).

Disadvantages of procurement without logistic

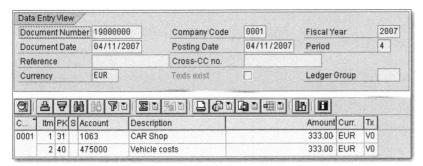

Figure 4.4 Accounting View of a Procurement Transaction from Accounts Payable Accounting

If you take a closer look at the document, significant documentation weaknesses become obvious when procurements without logistic are directly processed in the Financial Accounting (FI) component. For example, the document with the document number 19000000 only indicates that the documented procurement includes vehicle costs of $333.00. It does not provide any logistical information, for example, which commodities or services have actually been procured in what quantity and at what unit price. This information is only contained in the original document, which is usually provided in paper form.

This example shows that postings of procurement transactions entered directly in the Financial Accounting (FI) component primarily contain accounting-relevant information, such as the G/L account and values. Of course, you can enter additional information as text when you post expenditures directly in the Financial Accounting (FI) component. However, this is prone to errors because the content is based on the subjective evaluation of the accounting clerk. Moreover, entering supplementary text involves a great deal of effort and can be used in reports only to a limited extent. This is because, due to different input regarding content and orthography, grouping transaction data also is possible only to a limited extent. Consequently, in day-to-day business, supplementary text is rarely entered or only in exceptional situations.

A solely commercial documentation of procurements is not sufficient for two reasons. First, a lot of critical information on commodities and services procured is not entered and is thus not available for procurement controlling. As a result, you cannot analyze the procurement range and intensity, or, for that matter, the entire procurement controlling. In other words, it is not possible to control procurements in a strategic and operational manner.

Second, the process steps upstream from purchasing must be carried out outside the system, for example, the documentation of the legally binding contract with the vendor (purchase order), the technical verification of the invoice items, and the verification of the invoiced amount. This means that the entire procurement transaction is not "communicated" to the SAP system until a legally binding invoice has been received, which reduces flexibility. This is not really acceptable for the internal control and information system.

4.2.2 Entering Vendor Invoices in MM

Procurements without logistic can be posted under the invoice receipt directly to the G/L account, without reference. They can be processed in the MM component using Transaction MIRO (Enter Invoice).

You enter procurement transactions without reference directly to a G/L account in the same way as you enter them in the Financial Accounting (FI) component (see Figure 4.5). In this case, the procurement is again documented only on the basis of values, and without any logistical information – it therefore includes all resulting disadvantages with regard to reporting and procurement controlling.

Entry without reference to the G/L account

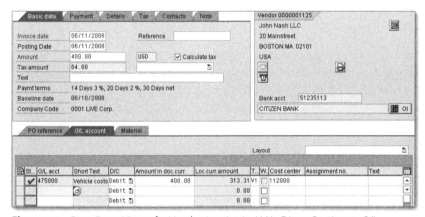

Figure 4.5 Data Entry View of a Vendor Invoice in MM; Direct Posting to G/L Account

However, exclusively using the MM component for procurements without logistic by directly posting them to G/L accounts is not reasonable because the same functions are already provided in the Financial Accounting (FI) component, which involves less Customizing and implementation effort. The direct posting from the MM component to G/L accounts is thus not economical and not further discussed here. In day-to-day business, however, you may want to use this function for organization and authorization purposes. The following sections place the processing procurements without logistic in the SAP system on the same level as the entry of incoming invoices in the Financial Accounting (FI) component.

4.2.3 Consequences for Procurements Without Logistic in Financial Accounting (FI)

For procurements without logistic, the process steps upstream of the vendor invoice are processed outside the SAP system, within the supply chain. Transactions, such as requirement requests, purchase orders, or goods receipts, are not processed in the SAP system and consequently not documented in the SAP system. This is a distinct disadvantage of this processing type. In the SAP system, the documentation of the operational processing of the entire procurement transaction is basic, fragmented, and not standardized. Critical process steps such as purchase orders are not entered in the SAP system at all. However, a purchase order is a legally binding request to a vendor to supply uniquely defined goods (commodities and services) in a specified quality and quantity, at a certain time, to a defined location, at a specific price.

Difficult purchase order monitoring

The monitoring of purchase orders is much more difficult when orders are not entered in the SAP system for procurements without logistic. If the responsible person is absent, it is, for example, quite difficult to verify the technical correctness of the goods delivery without adequate documentation. Defects can only be determined if the details (type, quality, location, time, and so on) of the purchase order are known. How are you supposed to verify that the delivery is correct if the system doesn't provide any purchase order information? Or how are you supposed to verify the invoice if no information on the goods receipt is available? In this case, it is nearly impossible to comply with the commercial obligation to give notice of defects because the purchaser of the goods has to give notice of the defects immediately after the service has been performed. Here, immediately means without undue delay. A delayed notification of the defect because there is no vacation replacement and purchase order information is missing may still be "without undue delay."

In the real world, these processing deficiencies are avoided by making bilateral oral agreements or by referring to purchase order documentation in emails or faxes that have been generated outside of the SAP system. However, this leads to integration gaps and problems regarding the internal control system. Because of unclear responsibilities, the risk of overlooking or omitting something is quite high in this processing variant.

The lack of commitments management is another disadvantage of procurement without logistic. Commitments comprise contractual obligations that lead to a flow of funds of comparable amounts in the near future. Commitment information missing from purchase orders prevents you from detecting — in good time – financial deficits or surpluses of liquid means. This is because current payables are not indicated in the SAP system for procurements without logistic until vendor invoices are entered (see Figure 4.6).

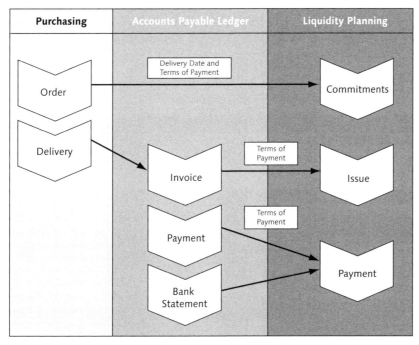

Figure 4.6 Liquidity Trend

In most cases, payables have to be paid within a few weeks. This time period, however, is too short for effective cash flow management and long-term financial budgeting. To eliminate these deficiencies, you can implement the Funds Management (SAP PSM) functions and create commitments using earmarked funds. The process of entering incoming invoices with reference to the respective earmarked funds results in a commitment reduction. However, you shouldn't underestimate the implementation and maintenance effort involved in an implementation of Funds Management. You need to define update rules from the SAP PSM component in Financial Accounting (FI), specify master data, and adapt to the ever-changing basic conditions.

No logistical documentation | Logistical documentation (material type, quantity, and so on) does not exist for procurements without logistic in the Financial Accounting (FI) component. It is impossible to implement procurement controlling with the goal of cross-organizational standardization of an item and service portfolio to utilize synergy effects and to ensure a reduction of follow-up and maintenance costs. The transaction is documented only on the basis of values in a G/L account. This is not detailed enough for procurement management or for controlling compliance with guidelines, and is thus unproductive. It also considerably limits the potential options of Financial Accounting (FI) Transaction FB60 (Enter Incoming Invoices).

Organizational responsibilities are not mapped | In addition, the risk of manipulation is high because there is no function for mapping organizational responsibilities to purchasing activities. The company code is the smallest organizational unit in the Financial Accounting (FI) component. Master data structures are made available for the documentation of procurements through the chart of accounts or through G/L accounts that are assigned to the company code. Consequently, you cannot implement the different purchasing types, for example, centralized, decentralized, or partially centralized, with reference to the different material groups.

Because of the existing deficiencies for processing procurements without logistic, particularly for entering incoming invoices directly in Financial Accounting (FI), you may wonder why this is significant at all (see Table 4.1). However, several reasons exist for its enormous relevance.

Advantages | The MM component is not implemented in every live SAP system. In particular, service providers with low procurement intensity and restricted procurement range do not want to make the effort necessary to implement the MM component. Without the MM functions, Transaction FB60 (Enter Incoming Invoices) is the only way of posting incoming invoices.

Reduced data entry effort | For goods with reduced procurement frequency, low procurement value (without complex internal approval processes), and simple purchase order handling – for example, filling out order forms on the Internet or in conventional catalogs – the data entry effort for purchase orders in MM is considered additional effort without benefit. In this case, only the vendor invoice is entered in the SAP system.

Ad-hoc procurements are processes where order, delivery, and payment are made at the same time. These processes usually occur in the consumer goods area and are also known as *impulse purchases*. Ad-hoc procurements result in directly delivered goods, receipts of the received goods, and completed cash or card payments. In this case, it doesn't make sense to enter the purchase orders in the SAP system because the objectives of the commitments documentation cannot be achieved. Therefore, only the vendor invoice or payment is posted.

Procurement processes without logistic are also used if material master records are missing, even if the MM functions are implemented and fully functional. You can enter incoming invoices using Transaction MIRO (Enter Invoices) with direct reference to material master records only if these master records exist. If the material master records weren't created during the implementation of the SAP system, you must create them during normal operation. This is a common procedure because requirements are dynamical and change over time. If master data is centrally managed with a request and approval system, the effort for requesting goods that are rarely procured is usually not made.

Consequently, vendor invoices are directly posted to G/L accounts, using either Transaction FB60 (Enter Incoming Invoices) in the Financial Accounting (FI) component, or Transaction MIRO (Enter Invoices) in the MM component. Compared to material master data, the chart of accounts is considerably less volatile in the long run. You can, for example, post procurements of toner cartridges for Canon and HP printers to the OFFICE SUPPLIES G/L account. In MM, this would require a master record with a lot of control information for each procurement.

Less volatility

The relatively high ratio of procurements without logistic in day-to-day business is often a result of the existing system landscape in the enterprise. For example, procurements are made in external systems and only consumption values are directly transferred to G/L accounts in the SAP system, via interfaces. If the data is then analyzed in the SAP system, a false impression arises.

External systems

Conclusion

The advantages of procurement processing in the Financial Accounting (FI) component are mainly a result of the reduced implementation effort. The relevant master data is restricted to G/L accounts, payment conditions, and payment methods. It belongs to the original master data of the Financial Accounting (FI) component and is an essential component of every SAP implementation. That means that no additional implementation and maintenance effort is required for procurement processes. The existing deficiencies regarding internal controls, commitments management, and documentation, however, require careful handling and clear specifications for this processing type.

You should allow for processing procurements without logistic in the SAP system only if the procurements meet the following criteria:

- They are approved exceptions
- They are trivial, without strategic character
- They are infrequent, with a low procurement value

To ensure this restrictive handling of procurements without logistic in the Financial Accounting (FI) component, you need to implement an appropriate organizational structure for procurements.

4.3 Procurement with Logistical Processing

For procurements with logistic, the MM component in the SAP system provides a wide range of functions. The goal is to cover all processes that are needed for system-supported material requirements planning, material procurement, inventory management, invoice verification, and material valuation.

The integrated processing of the entire procurement transaction in the SAP system, with complete logistical documentation, is the essential aspect of procurements with logistic. Table 4.2 lists the previously mentioned procurement applications and their respective tasks.

Application	Task
MM-CBP Material requirements planning	▶ Monitoring of stock levels ▶ Material requirements planning for production and sales ▶ Automatic or manual entry of material requirements
MM-PUR Purchasing	▶ External procurement of materials or services ▶ Internal procurement with relocation ▶ Determination of the best possible source of supply for requirements coverage ▶ Monitoring of delivery and payment dates ▶ Strategic procurement with bid invitations with contracts
MM-IM Inventory management	▶ Quantity-based and value-based management of the material stock ▶ Receipt of delivered products ▶ Return delivery of defective products ▶ Material withdrawal ▶ Transfer of material ▶ Reservation of material
QM-IM Quality inspection (in procurement)	▶ Inspection of goods receipts
LE-WMS Warehouse management	▶ Organization and storage bin-specific management of warehouse complexes ▶ Stock transfer of material ▶ Monitoring of all goods movements ▶ Physical inventory for each storage bin
MM-IV Invoice verification	▶ Entry of the vendor invoice and authorization of payment ▶ Verification of the vendor invoice with regard to content, price, and amounts

Table 4.2 Tasks of the Procurement Applications in SAP ERP

The following SAP system-technical and organizational prerequisites must be met to process procurements with logistic: You must maintain the master data that is necessary in MM, as well as the integration relationships of the MM components with other SAP components in the SAP system. You must also provide the organizational prerequisites for functional master data management (central or decentralized) and the corresponding document flow for purchasing processes.

The following sections describe the necessary prerequisites in greater detail.

4.3.1 Master Data

The existence of master data for the materials to be procured is a prerequisite for the system-supported purchasing of products in the SAP system's MM component. Master data is not changed by business processes, such as purchases or storage. Configuration of master data is consistent and usually influenced only by external conditions such as price or description changes on the vendor side. The opposite of master data is transaction data generated in business processes; accordingly it is volatile.

Material master record

The material master record in the SAP system contains different data for goods an enterprise procures on a regular basis. It enables detailed control of the documentation of procurement transactions (see Table 4.3).

Materials have a fundamental significance in the SAP system. Material master records determine the procurement range of an enterprise. This means, indirectly, that materials in all possible variations must be provided in the SAP system for the goods the enterprise requires – from office supplies to complex measuring devices. Otherwise, a system-supported procurement with appropriate documentation cannot be ensured.

Creating material master records

When the MM component is initially implemented in an enterprise, the implementation team first carries out a requirements analysis, which is usually quite time-consuming. The team then identifies and classifies the materials the enterprise needs. Next, it lays the foundation for a system-supported material supply by creating material master records in the SAP system. Right from go-live, all goods required by the enterprise can be procured ad hoc – and with system support – because all potential goods have an appropriate material master record in the SAP system. However, this optimal status doesn't last long because nothing is certain but change.

Dimension	Description
Purchasing	Purchasing data ensures efficient processing of purchases and is mandatory for the material master record. It includes specifications such as material descriptions, units of measure, weight, Universal Product Code (UPC), manufacturer part numbers, and so on.
Storage	Storage data is maintained only for materials that are subject to inventory management and is needed for inventory processing (storage, issue, material valuation, and so on). This includes data such as unit of issue, volume, hazardous material number, and so on.
Material requirements planning	Material requirements planning data is used for planning procurement activities and creates the prerequisites for a smooth supply of goods. Examples for material requirements planning data are reorder point, maximum stock level, minimum lot size, and so on.
Forecast	You can use forecast data to predict future material consumption based on past material consumption, using an appropriate forecasting technique. For this purpose, you have to enter the specifications of the forecasting technique, the seasonal index, and so on into the material master record.
Foreign trade Import	Foreign trade data is required to ensure efficient importation of goods, in accordance with customs authority regulations and official statistics requirements. Foreign trade data includes, for example, specifications on the country of origin or the statistical goods number for INTRASTAT and EXTRASTAT notifications for authorities.
Financial accounting	Financial accounting data enables you to update purchasing and transaction data to the relevant G/L accounts in the general ledger and is mandatory for every material master record. You can use the valuation class, for example, to post stock and consumption values for each material movement category to the corresponding G/L accounts. To evaluate the material, you can define whether a material master record is relevant for the LIFO and FIFO evaluation.
Sales	Sales data is only needed for materials that are resold as part of the business activity. Examples include the sales price and the minimum purchase quantity.

Table 4.3 Material Master Data Dimensions

Adapting material
master records In any enterprise, the requirements for goods are volatile and subject to constant change. Therefore, you must continually adapt the available material master records to the actual circumstances by creating new materials in the SAP system, using, for example, Transaction MM01 (Create Material) (see Figure 4.7).

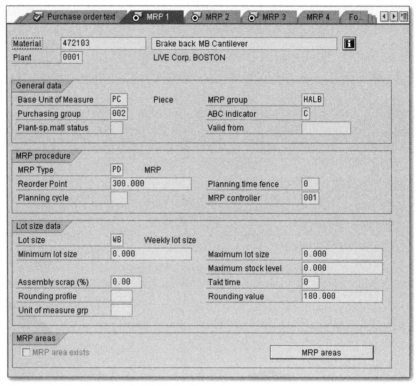

Figure 4.7 Creating a Material Master Record

You shouldn't underestimate the effort for creating materials manually. Due to the high integration depth in the SAP system, all components of the SAP logistics system use the material master record. That means that it provides about 440 potential input fields, distributed across 23 screens. The number of the data fields to be adapted depends on the areas where a material is supposed to be used. For example, if no goods are imported, you don't have to maintain the screen for importation. However, at least seven of the 440 potential input fields are mandatory. This means that you have to maintain at least seven configuration entries when you create a material in the SAP system. After you have defined a master record in the SAP system, you should conduct a detailed search in the entire dataset.

Only if you are certain that no appropriate master record exists, should you create a new one. This reduces the likelihood of a random proliferation of master records. Against this background, you should keep the manual maintenance effort for material master records in mind, and consider this as early as possible in the implementation phase of the MM component. The fundamental significance of materials requires an appropriate master record in the SAP system for each good that is supposed to be procured. This also means that you should provide one material master record for each variation of a good, for example, marker/green, marker/blue, marker/yellow. In some cases, the same item is defined in the system several times because it is procured from different vendors. This enables you to maintain the vendor item numbers used in purchase orders.

Manual maintenance effort

The effort involved could be kept to a minimum if you used configurable materials. In this case, you would create characteristics, classes, and configuration profiles for each configurable material (markers, envelopes, pens, and so on). In practice, however, configurable materials have not been accepted because of the high level of preliminary effort for the classification and the wide range of possible goods and their variants. This estimation is based on the retrograde analyses of more than 400 SAP operational clients, which have been carried out by IBIS Prof. Thome AG in the context of its business activities.

Configurable materials

Because configurable materials are not an accepted practice, you have to create an individual master record, or generic master records, for each material to be procured. Generic master records usually contain unspecific descriptions that are based mainly on the superordinate terms of the material classification. In the SAP system, you can create a generic material for all markers, for example. The purchaser can adapt the material description to his requirements when the material is selected during the entry of a purchase order or invoice.

The material description "marker," for example, can be changed to "marker, green" in the purchase order text. Problems occur when the definition of the reference material is not detailed enough so that the information is no longer available for subsequent procurement controlling. The system can only evaluate the consumption of markers; it does not consider the colors because they are not mentioned in the structured purchase order text. As an alternative to generic materials, you can also order materials via material groups. Here, you select a material group when you enter the purchase order or invoice and adapt the purchase order text according to the requirements.

Adapting the purchase order text

The flexibility regarding the adaption of the purchase order text leads to the risk that updates to the G/L accounts in Financial Accounting (FI) may be manipulated, and also involves a high potential for errors. For example, you could select the generic material, "PC requirements," and change the order text to "marker, green," which would result in wrong documentation of the actual procurement transaction because the update of the transaction data to the G/L accounts in Financial Accounting (FI) is based on the valuation class for PC requirements. This shows that the use of generic materials is clearly limited and that you can only use them for selected, low-value products. Consequently, individual master records are the only alternative to ensure sound, error-free, compliant documentation.

4.3.2 Integration

To ensure technically correct, integrated, and value-based updates of procurements in MM to the G/L accounts of the Financial Accounting (FI) component, during the SAP implementation, you have to implement settings for automatic postings to the G/L accounts in Financial Accounting (FI) and Cost Accounting for invoice receipts, transfer postings, or material movement in MM.

This is done by assigning valuation classes to G/L accounts (see Figure 4.8). A valuation class is comprised of a group of similar materials whose consumption or stock has to be documented on the same G/L account to comply with the Generally Accepted Accounting Principles with regard to the technically correct documentation of business transactions.

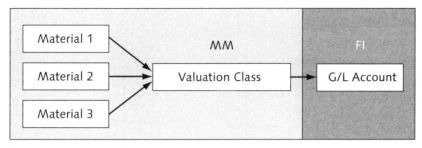

Figure 4.8 Valuation Class

The system settings lead to a framework that ensures that in an enterprise, all procurements with material reference are documented according to the same principles because the G/L account is determined when you select the material to be procured. Consequently, with operational processing of procurements, there is not much leeway with the technical documentation of procurements in external accounting.

4.3.3 Organization of Master Data Management

As already mentioned, you should consider the time-consuming and complex maintenance for material master records in the organizational structure. You can choose between two different types of master data management: central and decentralized.

In central master data management, you create master data for all purchasing departments at a central location in the enterprise. The wide range of configuration options clearly shows that you shouldn't leave material master data management to chance. Instead, before an enterprise implements the MM component, it should prepare a concept that defines how the different configurations are supposed to be managed.

Central master data management

Central master data management enables you to comply with these internal guidelines regarding master data maintenance in a particularly convenient way. It also helps avoid random proliferation of master data, and you end up with a dataset that meets enterprise-wide specifications and guidelines. Master data that doesn't meet operational requirements usually leads to a higher total cost of ownership (TCO). For example, duplicates in a master dataset lead to unnecessary search, reconciliation, and possibly reversal costs for operational processing if the wrong material is used in the purchase order. Consequently, TCO increases due to longer search times, reduced system ergonomics, and so on.

Disadvantages of central master data management Major disadvantages of central master data management are the complex communication paths and resulting time lag that arises because information is passed from decentralized purchasing departments to the central master data management center via faxes, Internet forms, emails, and so on. This organizational model is not suitable for time-critical requirements, where you have to react immediately to cover them.

Decentralized master data management In decentralized master data maintenance, purchasing departments that work operationally with the materials are responsible for updates. The advantages and disadvantages of this organizational model are diametrical to central management. Decentralized data maintenance ensures short reaction times to new requirements. Due to the definition of the required materials in the SAP system, each purchasing department can place purchase orders without time delay, ensuring a timely goods supply.

Combinations Which organizational model you select depends on the company's organization. A "pure" central or decentralized organization is rarely found. A combination of both, for example, is material group-oriented partial centralization. Here, master data authorization is centralized for selected material groups. The material responsibility for the remaining material groups stays with the purchasing departments. This enables you, for example, to centrally manage complex goods, such as PCs or vehicles. These are strategic in nature, and their purchasing is supposed to be standardized within the enterprise. Individual purchasing departments can enter convenience goods or goods with high volatility in a decentralized way and then procure them.

The use of the MM component in day-to-day business is limited by the rather time-consuming and organizationally complex management of materials when the requirements are highly volatile and if a wide range of variants exists. Depending on the enterprise-internal master data management (central/decentralized) and the organizational structure, the purchasing processing may be considerably restricted (see Section 4.3.7, Criteria for Procurements with Logistic in MM).

4.3.4 Document Flow with Regard to Purchasing

In the SAP ERP system, the functional tasks of applications are controlled and processed via documents. In core processes, such as material procurement, they represent individual consecutive subprocesses.

For the document flow in SAP systems, data is automatically transferred from preceding documents to logically subsequent documents. For example, a purchase order is generated with reference to a purchase requisition, and the data is transferred from the existing requisition. This ensures the consistency of the data used in the process flow with regard to content, and accelerates the document flow (see Figure 4.9).

Automatic data transfer

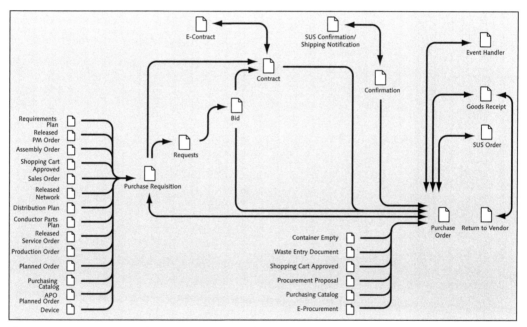

Figure 4.9 Procurement in the SAP ERP System with Upstream and Downstream Processes

Depending on the preceding document, in MM the SAP system distinguishes between the following types of invoice receipts:

Types of invoice receipts

▶ Entering incoming invoices without reference

▶ Entering incoming invoices with reference to a purchase order

▶ Entering incoming invoices with reference to a goods receipt

4.3.5 Entering Vendor Invoices Without Reference

Procurements without reference are characterized by the fact that incoming invoices are entered without reference to preceding documents, for example, purchase order or goods receipt.

Entering invoices manually

System-supported procurement processing in the SAP system starts with manually entering the vendor invoice. Subsequent processes – such as automatic outgoing payments – access the control data of the posted vendor invoice (payment path and payment conditions) and are processed without additional manual intervention (see Figure 4.10).

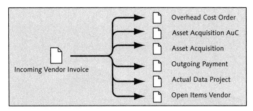

Figure 4.10   Vendor Invoice Without Reference

You can enter invoices without reference in the MM component in two ways:

▸ Directly to the G/L account

▸ With reference to a material master record

You can use Transaction MIRO (Enter Invoice) for both processing types.

Entry directly to the G/L account

In MM, entering vendor invoices directly to a G/L account is also known as *purchase order with user-defined text*. It corresponds to the scope of functions in the component and is described in Section 4.2, Procurement Without Logistical Processing.

Entry with reference to the material master record

The second option – entering incoming invoices with direct reference to materials – is one of the core functions of the MM component and is often used in day-to-day business. The average percentage of use of this procurement type is about 10% of all procurement items processed via the MM component. This estimate also rests upon the retrograde analyses of more than 400 SAP operational clients, which have been carried out by IBIS Prof. Thome AG in the context of its business activities.

Entering vendor invoices without reference is based on the invoice submitted to the purchaser (original paper document, fax, email, and so on). When you enter the invoice, the vendor's information (material number, description, size, and so on) is transferred to the enterprise-internal information framework. The purchaser does this manually by entering the corresponding material numbers into the SAP entry screen for the invoice items listed on the document (see Figure 4.11). By storing the invoice, the system generates a corresponding MM and Financial Accounting (FI) document.

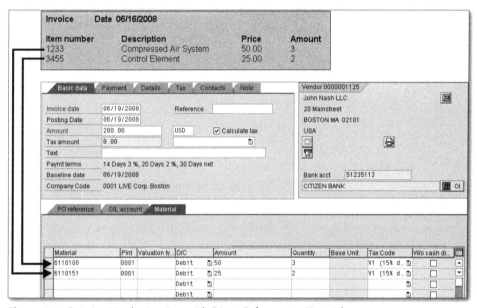

Figure 4.11 Entering Vendor Invoices with Direct Reference to Material

If the appropriate master records are missing, you cannot enter the invoice. This again emphasizes the fundamental significance of the material master records, on the one hand, and the requirements for the purchaser, on the other hand. The purchaser needs to know the materials that exist in the SAP system to find the corresponding master records. In Figure 4.11, for example, an invoice for 50 pieces of material 6110100 and 25 pieces of material 6110151 has been entered. For inexperienced readers, these cryptic material numbers don't provide any information. However, a professional purchaser who knows the logical structure of the material master data in the system can see at glance that these are materials from different number ranges and thus materials with different significance for the enterprise

Knowing the logical structure makes it much easier for the specialized purchaser to search in the dataset. However, the number of existing material master records often exceeds 100,000. To reduce the search effort, there are 24 different search helps that, for example, search for:

▶ Material number/description

▶ Material with bill of material

▶ Competing products of competitors

▶ Material of a class

▶ Material of a material group

▶ Material of a material category

▶ Material of a European article number

▶ Material of a manufacturer number

The result of a correctly deployed search help is a significantly reduced dataset from which you can select the appropriate material (see Figure 4.12).

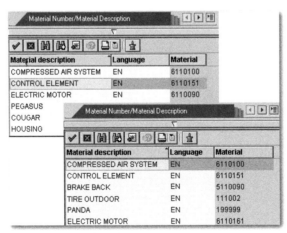

Figure 4.12 Search Helps

Compared to entering vendor invoices in the Financial Accounting (FI) component, the main advantage of this solution is the detailed logistical documentation. By entering the material in the invoice item, the system automatically provides all attributes that have been maintained for this material in the master data management, such as description, unit of measure, and price, which reduces the data entry effort considerably. Furthermore, the data is then available for procurement controlling as well.

If vendor invoices are entered without reference in the SAP system, all upstream process steps within the supply chain (for example, purchase order or goods receipt) have been carried out outside the SAP system. In this context, this processing type has the same disadvantages as procurements without logistical processing (see Section 4.2, Procurement Without Logistical Processing). The monitoring of purchase orders is a lot more difficult when the purchase order does not exist in the SAP system. It also affects commitments management and makes it possible to violate compliance guidelines.

Disadvantages of entries without references

Conclusion

The relatively high percentage of vendor invoices without references (20% of all invoices entered in the component) emphasizes the significance of this processing type in day-to-day business. The system-supported processing type is usually used for ad-hoc procurements that cannot be planned. This includes, for example, fueling vehicles, or the unexpected procurement of spare parts. In this case, it would be counterproductive to enter the purchase order in the SAP system first and then procure the ordered goods. Entering vendor invoices without reference in the SAP system is thus a pragmatic solution for procurements that cannot be planned, while maintaining high documentation quality at the same time.

4.3.6 Entering Vendor Invoices with Reference

The main characteristic of system-supported procurements with reference is that entering vendor invoices takes place at the end of the supply chain.

The document flow in the SAP system enables you to transfer data from preceding documents to logically subsequent documents. When you

Transferring data

59

enter vendor invoices, the reference to preceding documents reduces the data that has to be entered in the system considerably (see Figure 4.13).

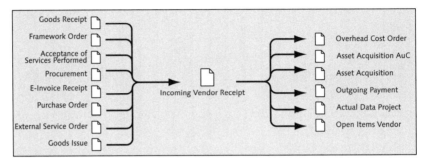

Figure 4.13 Vendor Invoice with Reference

When you enter a vendor invoice with reference to a purchase order using Transaction MIRO (Enter Invoices), you have to, for example, copy the following specifications from the vendor invoice:

▸ Invoice date (issue date of the incoming invoice)

▸ Posting date (any date to determine the posting period)

▸ Gross invoice amount

▸ Purchase order number

▸ If required, the invoice number of the vendor in the Reference field (see Figure 4.14)

▸ You also have to activate the Calculate Tax field

By entering the data mentioned in this list, particularly the purchase order number, the system transfers the individual items from the referenced order to the invoice. With this process, you don't have to transfer the information framework of the vendor invoice (material number, description, size, and so on) to the internal information framework, as you have to do for invoice entries without reference.

In Figure 4.14, for example, five items, including all details such as quantity, input tax code, and so on, have been automatically transferred from purchase order 4500000883 to the vendor invoice that needs to be entered.

In this context, the purchaser or accounts payable accountant must determine the arithmetical correctness by comparing the items from the vendor's invoice with the individual purchase order items proposed by the system and verifying whether the quantity and price specifications are correct. If there are no differences, the purchaser can confirm the individual items by clicking on them. If the purchaser determined deviations to the disadvantage of the enterprise between the purchase order and invoice, or if the corresponding goods receipt is missing, the purchaser blocks the invoice.

Checking the arithmetical correctness

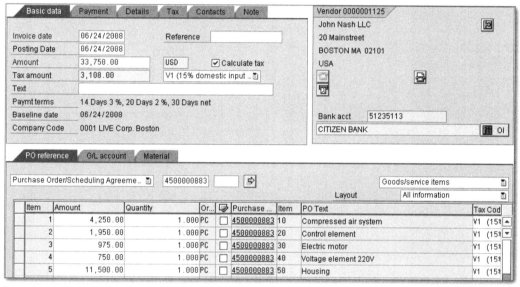

Figure 4.14 Entering the Vendor Invoices with Direct Reference to a Purchase Order

The technical correctness is checked when the goods receipt is posted, based on the delivery note. You can also use Transaction MIGO (Goods Receipt Purchase Order) to post the goods receipt with reference to the purchase order. By referencing the purchase order, you only need to transfer certain specifications from the delivery note to the SAP system:

Checking the technical correctness

▶ Document date (issue date of the delivery note)

▶ Posting date (any date to determine the posting period)

▶ Delivery note number

▶ Purchase order number

When you have entered the purchase order number and transferred the proposed dates to the document and posting date, the system copies the goods receipt items from the purchase order to the goods receipt document for posting. The goods receipt quantities have to be transferred from the delivery note (see Figure 4.15).

Figure 4.15 Entering the Goods Receipt

The technical invoice verification is very efficient if all purchase order information is available. Thus, you can easily comply with the commercial obligation to give notice of defects. The person responsible has to check the goods delivered and compare the items listed on the delivery note with the purchase order items in terms of quantity and content. You can click on **OK** to confirm the technical correctness (see Figure 4.15). If you determine deviations that go beyond the tolerance limits defined in Customizing, you cannot post the goods receipt.

As mentioned previously, entry transactions for vendor invoices and goods receipts with reference to purchase orders are used only for confirmation purposes and involve a low level of data entry effort. The purchase order is the central information object for procurements with reference and can be deployed in different procurement processes. You can procure materials for direct consumption, warehousing, or services. The SAP system logs subsequent activities of purchase orders, such as goods or invoice receipt, so you can monitor the procurement transaction at any time (see Figure 4.16).

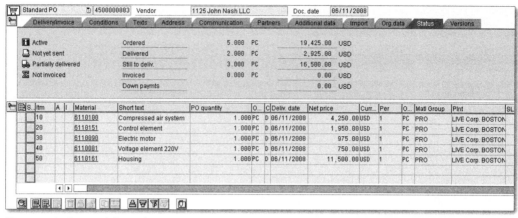

Figure 4.16 Status of the Ordering Transaction

Purchase orders can be entered into the SAP system in different ways. This depends on whether the process documents preceding the ordering transaction, such as purchase requisition (PReq), request, contract, manufacturing order, and so on, are specified in the SAP system. The following text doesn't discuss these process types, but focuses on the standard purchase order, that is, the manual purchase order entry without preceding documents.

You can use the following two transactions to manually enter purchase order information into the SAP system:

Manually entering purchase order information

▶ ME21N (Vendor/Delivering Plant Known)

▶ ME25 (Vendor Unknown)

Irrespective of whether the vendor is known or unknown, you must enter all of the information relevant for the purchase order. Because purchase orders are legally binding documents with a high integration depth on the system side, the number of specifications needed is quite high, even for standard purchase orders. By default, there are ten tabs at the document header level and eleven additional tabs at the level of the document items, which can be used to enter purchase order information (see Figure 4.17).

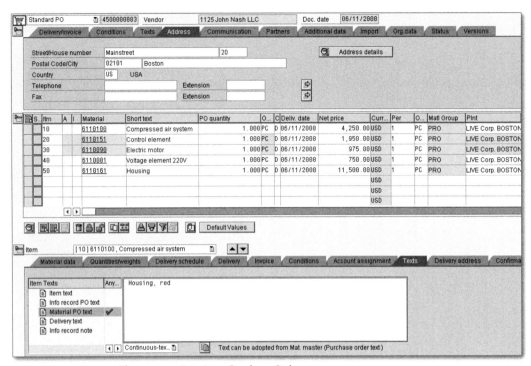

Figure 4.17 Entering a Purchase Order

By entering various specifications, you ensure that the ordering transaction and information flow to the vendor and to subsequent documents will be smooth. You can, for example, add information to the material description proposed by the system that is critical for the vendor. This information might include delivery instructions or vendor material descriptions, and can accelerate purchase order processing at the vendor.

Conclusion

Procurements with completely system-supported logistical processing require you to formalize the data entry to enable automatic processing of the individual steps within the supply chain and controlling using appropriate reporting. This formalization, in turn, leads to multiplication of the data volume. Instead of writing the text "housing, red, 3 pieces" onto the purchase order or fax, you have to enter four different specifications when data is processed automatically. This is both an advantage and disadvantage for this variant of procurement processing in the SAP system.

The advantages include the detailed documentation of the operational processing of the entire procurement transaction, the creation of a sound, detailed data basis for procurement controlling, and the integration into Financial Accounting with an early provision of the information for commitments management. The major disadvantages that restrict the use of the *vendor invoice entry with reference* in day-to-day business are the high complexity despite the information that can be stored in purchase information and material master records, and the high level of data entry effort for purchase orders that is linked to the degree of customization (foreign purchase, customs formalities, dangerous goods procurement) of various procurement transactions. This functional power of the SAP ERP system requires the knowledge of an experienced purchaser. That means clear limitations are placed on the use for occasional users.

Manually entering purchase order information

Despite the wide range of functions the SAP ERP system provides, you cannot, in reality, expect that a purchase order is entered in the SAP system that comprises ten tabs at the header level and eleven at the item level and, depending on the connection to the vendor, that must be printed and faxed to the vendor – only to order a marker, or toner for a printer. This is especially true if you consider that before the implementation of the SAP system, you only had to manually fill out a purchase order note or write a fax or email. The advantages of integrated data processing for upstream process steps and enabled procurement controlling are difficult to communicate because of the significantly high level of data entry effort.

High level of effort

Before you implement the procurements with reference process variant, you should analyze the procurement range in detail to determine the appropriate goods for this procurement type. Procurements with logistical processing in the SAP system don't represent a comprehensive solution concept for all procurement areas. You should use this function primarily for strategically critical, complex, and high-quality goods with potential enterprise-internal synergy effects and high order frequency and quantity. These properties of goods lead to the procurement characteristics listed in Table 4.4.

Property	Characteristic
Origin of requirements	Cyclical/central/plannable
Purchase order quantity	High
Purchase order value	High
Vendor strategy	Single sourcing
Procurement process	Not standardized, heterogeneous requirements

Table 4.4 Properties of the Goods for SAP ERP-Controlled Procurement

These properties lead to numerous plannable activities preceding the purchase order, for example, market surveys, awards of contract, and so on, and subsequent activities, such as accepting or enforcing claims under warranty. The SAP system provides comprehensive functions to carry out these tasks.

4.3.7 Criteria for Procurements with Logistic in MM

As mentioned in Section 4.3.1, Master Data, the *procurement with logistical processing* process is dependent primarily on the existence of appropriate master data. Due to the high level of integration and volatility, master data maintenance is a significant cost driver for process costs.

Conditions for procurement with SAP MM

Consequently, the creation of a new material master, and thus the use of procurements with logistical processing, should depend on the following aspects:

▶ Order frequency

▶ Cumulative classification

▶ Requirement for inventory management

It makes sense to create a material master record when you can expect that the material has to be procured at least twelve times a year, for example. If the minimum yearly cumulative classification is $10,000, for example, you should consider creating a material master. If a material is subject to inventory management, you have to maintain a master record for system-supported procurement processing, the storage processes, and the use in production. For materials that are subject to inventory management, the stock is valuated by the system and identified on the balance sheet. The exact characteristics of the previously mentioned criteria, however, should be defined individually for each enterprise. You can't specify any default settings.

If you can't meet the previously discussed criteria, you shouldn't create a material master because the level of effort involved is too high. However, to be able to process system-supported procurements with logistic, you should use generic materials or purchase orders without material master records.

In summary, you can say that procurement processing with the functions of the MM component in the SAP system is mainly suited for professional and experienced purchasers and not for occasional purchasers. The numerous necessary specifications require detailed process knowledge and sometimes even accounting expertise. The complexity in the application and the time-consuming master data maintenance restrict the use of the introduced functions to complex, non-standardized, and strategically critical procurement transactions.

5 Implementing Procurement Processing in SAP SRM

This chapter deals with the options of Internet-based procurement using SAP's Supplier Relationship Management solution (SAP SRM). As described in Chapter 4, Implementing Procurement Processing in SAP ERP, the functions of the SAP ERP system don't enable you to process all possible procurement transactions efficiently and supported by the system. The following sections show you how you can close the existing functional gaps of the SAP ERP system using SAP SRM to offer appropriate software support for the entire range of procurement transactions within the SAP world.

5.1 Goals of E-Procurement

The main goal of e-procurement is to cut down process costs by reducing processing and lead times. Reducing procurement costs by grouping requirements and classifying vendors is only a subordinate goal.

In e-procurement, you cut down process costs mainly by providing a goods catalog that complies with general enterprise-internal guidelines. All authorized consumers may then use this catalog. This considerably reduces procurement-immanent tasks, such as searches, initiations, negotiations, and purchase order handling, particularly for products with high order frequency.

Goods catalog

Consequently, goods and services that are frequently ordered and involve a high and decentralized distributed number of purchasing agents are best suited for electronic procurement. However, the goods and services must be uniquely defined so that they can be listed in electronic catalogs (for example, DIN and standard parts such as screws). Section 5.2, Goods Catalog, shows how these materials can be listed in goods catalogs and describes the aspects you have to consider when maintaining and using

Suited goods

the catalog data. Next, the internal and external connection options for this content are introduced. Based on these principles, Section 5.4, Strategic Procurement Management, discusses strategic procurement management aspects. Sections 5.5, Operational Procurement Processing, and 5.6, Prerequisites for Procurement Processing with SAP SRM, detail the effects for operational procurement processing and the prerequisites for implementing this with SAP SRM.

5.2   Goods Catalog

The goods catalog is an integral component of any e-procurement solution. Its significance is identical to that of material master data in the MM component of the SAP ERP system. You cannot use Internet-based procurement without the catalog.

Strategic and operational purchasing
The goods catalog represents the first stage of any procurement process in an SAP SRM system and is located at the interface between strategic and operational purchasing (see Figure 5.1).

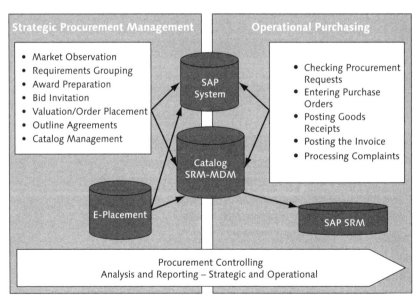

Figure 5.1   E-Procurement

The catalog management software must therefore consider the goals of the strategic and operational purchaser.

Catalog Management Systems

The e-procurement solution of SAP SRM does not depend on a specific catalog management system and can interact with various catalog systems via Open Catalog Interface (OCI). Purchasers can use OCI to call catalogs in the SAP SRM system via a browser, search for the appropriate products, transfer the goods to the shopping cart, and trigger the purchase order.

Open catalog interface

This way, the SAP SRM operator can deploy a catalog system that meets his requirements.

Over time, SAP has offered different catalog management systems together with the SRM solution by default. First, SAP provided the product *Requisite Catalog* by Requisite Technology. In 2004/2005, SAP changed its strategy and provided its own catalog management system, *SAP Catalog & Content Management System* (SAP CCM), Version 2.0. It was included in SAP SRM's scope of licenses. However, this solution did not establish itself in the market. So in June 2006, its development ceased.

The catalog management system currently delivered by SAP with SAP SRM is a subcomponent of SAP NetWeaver Master Data Management (SAP NetWeaver MDM) and is called *SRM-Master Data Management* (SRM-MDM). There are no additional license costs for SRM-MDM. The SRM-MDM catalog software is currently available in Version 2.0.

SAP SRM-MDM

Because SAP SRM doesn't provide proprietary catalogs, the following sections generically describe tasks, functions, and requirements for the catalog management system. In SAP SRM, you define the catalogs using the Customizing module Define External Web Services (catalogs, list of vendors, and so on), as a web service (see Figure 5.2).

Figure 5.2 Defining the Catalogs in SAP SRM

Web services are software applications that can be uniquely identified on the Internet. Therefore, to call a service or catalog, you have to maintain the calling parameters needed to find the service (see Figure 5.3). You can use the CALL STRUCTURE STANDARD for all catalogs. The service is called in a separate browser window. The integrated call structure ensures that the service is activated within the SRM application. You should use this application if you deploy the catalog management systems provided by SAP. Currently, this only applies to the SRM-MDM catalog management system.

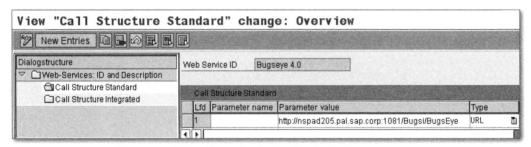

Figure 5.3 Calling Parameter for the Goods Catalog

Web service categories The configuration requirements for the web service depend on the business category. It defines the technical functionality and Customizing of the service in the SRM server and determines which web services are available for which SRM server applications (purchasing, bid invitations, requests, supplier self services, and so on). SAP SRM distinguishes between the following types of web services: product catalog, list of vendors, e-form, list of service providers, vendor evaluation, vendor pre-selection, project system. The following list describes selected business types in greater detail:

▶ **Product catalog**
You can use the product catalog to integrate regular catalog management systems. You should integrate all catalogs that support OCI.

▶ **E-form**
This type has the same properties as the product catalog but ensures the transfer of additional, freely definable product supplements from the server to the web service. For example, when you order anniversary presents, you can transfer text for the engraving.

▶ **Vendor list**
Supports the integration of vendor lists that have an Open Partner Interface (OPI) into SAP SRM. This enables you to directly transfer business partner data to the application components, for example, request or bid invitation.

For product catalogs, in addition to the obligatory technical settings, you can also configure selected functions in the SRM server and catalog management systems (see Figure 5.4).

The additionally provided functions in the product catalogs are derived from the interfaces between the catalog management system and the SAP SRM system. Usually, the ordering transaction starts by identifying the product in the catalog and is completed by transferring the item to the shopping cart in the SAP SRM and thus ordering it. In some situations, the ordering process can start in the SAP SRM system. However, in this case, you must return to the catalog.

Functions of the product catalog

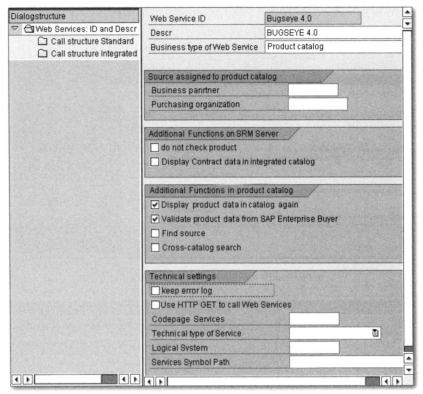

Figure 5.4 Configuration of the Product Catalog in SAP SRM

By activating the function DISPLAY PRODUCT DATA IN CATALOG AGAIN, you can considerably improve the operational usability of e-procurement. If you don't activate this field, the system displays the product details, such as description, technical details, and so on, only during the product search in the catalog. When you have selected the item and transferred it to the shopping cart in the SAP SRM system, only the purchase order-relevant data, such as item number, price, quantity, and so on, is displayed. If you activate this function, you can navigate from the purchase order in the SAP SRM system to the catalog again (see Figure 5.1) to have the system display detailed information on the selected product in the shopping cart. The user can use the PROCESS PURCHASE ORDERS function to have the system display detailed product information in the catalog, for example, technical specifications for the individual shopping cart items.

Using the Find Source function, you can trigger a vendor search in the catalog directly from the purchase order in the SAP SRM system. This may be necessary when an existing shopping cart has to be revised. In this case, the user can assign new sources of supply to the existing shopping cart items with the Process Purchase Orders function.

The VALIDATE PRODUCT DATA FROM SAP ENTERPRISE BUYER function is also interface-dependent. By activating this function, you can return from the SAP SRM system to the catalog. This is required for SRM-triggered purchase orders, if you work with templates. In this case, by returning to the catalog after the purchase order item has been transferred from the template to the shopping cart, you can check whether the catalog still contains the shopping cart items or products and determine price deviations. The cross-catalog search is significant only when several catalogs are connected to the SAP SRM system. The catalogs used must support the functions mentioned.

5.2.1 Creating and Maintaining Catalog Data

The central task of catalog software is to organize and manage different product data. For this purpose, product data of different vendors from different catalogs is transferred to a homogenous structure using the Content Load Workbench in order to provide the data in different output formats for the relevant processes (see Figure 5.5).

Managing product data

Consequently, the in-house catalog or its content (that is used in the enterprise) determines the procurement range of the enterprise, just as the material master records do in the SAP ERP system. Alternatively or additionally, you can connect external catalogs to SAP SRM, either directly from the vendor or via market places. The integration of material master data from the SAP ERP system is mandatory for items that are subject to inventory management (see Section 5.3.2, Internal Integration).

Material master data

The catalog management software provides several functions, including product data maintenance, navigation within the product portfolio, and detailed presentation of the items. The maintenance functions are primarily provided for the strategic purchaser, who is responsible for a cross-organizational standardization and homogenization of the item and

Product data maintenance

service portfolio to utilize synergy effects, and for reducing follow-up and maintenance costs.

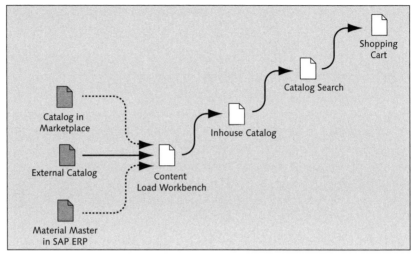

Figure 5.5 Creating a Catalog

Based on the decision about the products to be listed in the catalog, you can carry out these tasks very efficiently. By filling the in-house catalog with product data, goods consumption in an enterprise can be actively influenced without complex communications paths. The strategic purchaser has freely definable options. He can use different catalogs and, for example, transfer items of different manufacturers to the schema of a single catalog. For this purpose, the strategic purchaser uses the Content Management tools and decides which products from which catalogs are published in the in-house catalog, and in which form.

Comparing vendors
This lets you directly compare items from different vendors because all of the offers from various vendors are listed together. For example, the COPY PAPER material group in the in-house catalog includes all corresponding items. This lets you provide a sufficient overview of all existing items and the highest market transparency. With this process, the in-house catalog is filled with items that correspond to the enterprise's requirements range at the material group level. This type of data retention places high demands on the catalog software because it must trans-

form complex and multi-tier content into a standardized catalog data format.

The maintenance of catalog data refers primarily to entering new products and updating existing data, such as price updates. The following parties may maintain the data:

Who maintains catalog data?

- ▶ The enterprise
- ▶ A service provider
- ▶ The vendor

You should consider using the first alternative if the number of vendors whose data has to be integrated into the goods catalog doesn't exceed certain limits. This is because currently most of the vendors provide their catalog data in different digital formats. To integrate it into the catalog of the enterprise procuring the goods, the data must be converted to a compatible format. If several vendors are involved, this results in a high level of integration and maintenance effort. In this case, the purchasing resources that are released by using e-procurement are consumed again by the maintenance of the catalog. Because of the Content Management complexity, individual enterprises quickly face major challenges and financial burdens.

Maintaining catalogs yourself

For comprehensive vendor portfolios, you should transfer the maintenance effort to a service provider. Such an intermediary, also called *content broker*, is provided with the non-standardized data of all vendors and integrates it into the collective catalog of the enterprise procuring the materials. The use of intermediaries may also be required for security reasons if individual vendors shouldn't access the in-house catalog system to maintain the data directly.

Content broker

The significance of catalog service providers has increased considerably over time because the number of the necessary price and item updates positively correlates with the number of the existing vendors in the catalog. However, you must also consider that the services of content brokers incur costs. Therefore, you should make the respective make-or-buy decisions based on a conventional profitability analysis.

Even with content broker services, it would be unrealistic to claim that enterprises that use e-procurement don't have to do anything to manage the catalog. For example, during the Content Management process, enterprises have to check the provided items for relevance and, if required, remove unnecessary or undesired products when a new vendor catalog is approved (see Figure 5.6).

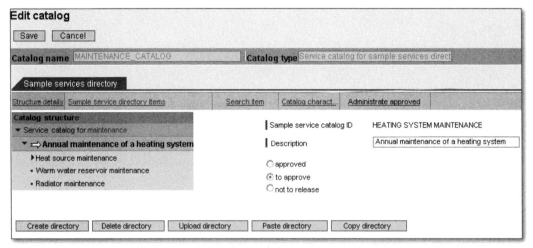

Figure 5.6 Approving the Catalog Items

In addition, you must check the catalog content for goods that must be capitalized, and select the relevant items as "to be capitalized." This ensures that the fixed asset accountant is integrated automatically into the workflow process during the procurement, or when the shopping cart is composed in the SAP SRM system. Therefore, you should have a clear idea of the internal activities required for catalog management as early as possible, and you should build up your own knowledge for performing the respective tasks to avoid unpleasant surprises in live operation.

Direct connection of vendor catalogs

As an alternative to an in-house catalog, whose content can be influenced by the enterprise, you can connect catalogs of different vendors directly to the SAP SRM system via OCI. The advantage of this solution consists of the complete externalization of the catalog management costs, while simultaneously updating the product information (prices, availability, and so on). In this case, however, the strategic purchasing department gives up the controllability of consumption. Consequently, you should only consider the connection of vendor catalogs to the in-house catalog as an additional option, and restrict it to selected vendors with special requirements, such as, for example, books.

Product Classification

When structuring the in-house catalog, or categorizing products hier-archically, you shouldn't reinvent the wheel by developing individual material groups and structuring them hierarchically. Instead, you should decide on a standard early on, to ensure a flexible exchange of product or catalog data with vendors and to achieve a high hit ratio for product searches in catalogs. This is an important advantage compared with the conventional master data organization in the SAP ERP system.

By using the most widespread uniform standards in this area, for example eCl@ss or Standard Products and Services Classification (UN/SPSC), the enterprise can benefit from the extensive experience of the operating organizations when categorizing products.

UN/SPSC is a classification concept that has been developed by the United Nations. Goods are categorized using five levels: segment, family, class, commodity, and business function. The fifth level includes the business relationship. This enables an internal analysis of different products and business relationships. The advantage of this standard consists of the global usability of the classification. The UN/SPSC standard is available in ten languages and contains 20,000 classified goods categories from five different segments, from raw materials to services (*www.unspsc.org*).

eCl@ss is a standard that has been developed by leading German enter-prises for the product classification of materials, products, and services. This standard is characterized by a hierarchically structured keyword register and a corresponding, four-stage material classification key that uniquely identifies each keyword. There are four hierarchy stages for classification, functional area, main group, group, and subgroup. The classification key provides two figures for each stage. Classifying prod-ucts according to eCl@ss lets you search by keyword(s), classification number, or item hierarchy (see Figure 5.7).

Categorizing material groups

UN/SPSC

eCl@ss

Figure 5.7 Material Groups at eClass

User-friendly, intuitive, and quick product identification in catalogs defines the success of the e-procurement system. An accurate search in catalogs is possible when the characteristics the catalog operators use to classify the products are identical with the search criteria the people carrying out the search use.

> **Example**
>
> This example illustrates how complex and multi-faceted the requirements for a product classification are. Inexperienced users could assign the Uncoated Paper item subgroup either to the Office Paper or to the Handicraft Paper material group. Due to the existing and expected product characteristics of the Uncoated Paper item subgroup, it is actually assigned to the Handicraft Paper material group. This enables a more precise product identification by the person who conducts the search (see Figure 5.8).

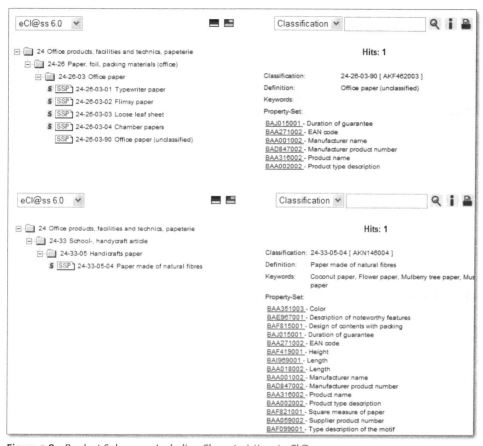

Figure 5.8 Product Subgroups Including Characteristics at eCl@ss

By complying with widespread standards for the goods classification, you can minimize communication problems during data exchanges, increase the hit ratio for the product identification, and reduce the effort for catalog maintenance and creation at the same time. In powerful content management systems, you can use several additive classification concepts, for example, eCl@ss and UN/SPSC.

5.2.2   Using Catalog Data

To achieve the primary goal of a shortened procurement process using e-procurement, you must structure the subarea of the product selection efficiently, which represents one of the most time-consuming and thus

Requirements for the catalog

cost-intensive areas. A prerequisite for this is that the items that cover the requirements are clearly displayed to quickly find them. If you use a digital catalog, the homogenous product search and secure navigation are evaluation criteria for the system's user friendliness and usability.

From the user's point of view, you must meet the following requirements:

▶ **Search mechanisms**
The first characteristic is powerful search mechanisms: The wide range of catalog data requires various search algorithms, stop lists, search authorizations, characteristics search, full-text search, hierarchical search, and so on. This emphasizes the benefits of electronic catalogs in SAP SRM compared to material master management in the SAP ERP system. The search mechanisms are much more powerful, and enable quick and efficient identification of the materials that are supposed to be procured. By default, the SAP ERP system only provides 24 search helps and doesn't include a hierarchical search or characteristics search.

▶ **Performance**
Performance is the second criterion: Due to the wide range of possible items in the catalog, the load performance should be at least 1,000 master records per minute.

▶ **Multi client capability**
Multi client capability is the third characteristic: The goods catalog should be able to supply several installations of SAP SRM.

▶ **Archiving**
Finally, you should provide useful archiving: It should be possible to outsource historical data.

5.3   Integration

The integration capability of SAP SRM is an essential prerequisite for its success. The integration directions are versatile because the e-procurement solutions are usually integrated into already existing system landscapes and access data and functions of existing application systems.

The SAP SRM system is configured in the same way as the SAP ERP system using the Implementation Guide, also called *IMG*. You can call the IMG using Transaction SPRO.

From Release SAP ERP 6.0 on, you can integrate SAP SRM as an add-on into the SAP system landscape. The variant requires that the SAP SRM server is installed in the same client as SAP ERP. In this case, SAP SRM and SAP ERP share the technical platform (see Figure 5.9).

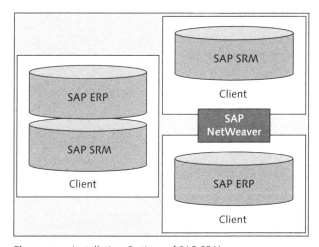

Figure 5.9 Installation Options of SAP SRM

However, this resource-friendly variant involves functional restrictions. For example, procurement activities in SAP SRM can only be supported for one backend system (see Section 5.3.2, Internal Integration). Conversely, this means that you cannot implement SAP SRM as a hub for the cross-SAP ERP group of requirement requests and their implementation as purchase orders.

These functional restrictions are not generally applicable and have to be evaluated for each enterprise specifically. For enterprises with only one live client, the add-on variant is quite acceptable to reduce operating costs and enable the use of e-procurement. However, you have to consider the future viability: You cannot update or migrate a separately installed SAP SRM system. The significance of this restriction may increase when additional SAP ERP clients emerge in the area of responsibility of the enterprise through acquisitions and mergers.

Installation in
separate clients The second alternative for integrating the SAP SRM server into the SAP system landscape is the installation in a separate client. This variant involves higher operating costs but provides a higher level of integration security and flexibility as a hub implementation for the integration of backend systems. This lets you fully benefit from the advantages of e-procurement resulting from the centralization of strategic tasks and the complete decentralization of operational purchasing management.

Because SAP SRM is located at the interface between the internal backend systems and vendor systems, a distinction is made between external and internal integration.

5.3.1 External Integration

External integration refers to the integration of vendors or service providers with the SAP SRM system. It is the basic prerequisite for a consistent data flow within electronic procurement processes. In the context of external integration, when integrating vendors you have to consider master or catalog data as well as transaction data.

Integrating the Catalog Data

Changes regarding
items

The system-based transfer of catalog data is essential for the creation of electronic catalogs because you cannot manually implement all changes made to items by vendors, for example, regarding prices or item descriptions. For this reason, general standards assume an important role for the classification of products and services.

For the integration of catalog data, there is no uniform standard available to exchange multimedia product and catalog data between all catalog management systems of vendors and procuring or SAP SRM-operating enterprises.

BMEcat

Most enterprises provide their catalog data in, for example, EDI or XML format. The BMEcat format has the potential to become the most important standard for transferring product catalog data in German-speaking countries. BMEcat is an XML-based exchange format that has been specifically defined by the German Association Materials Management, Purchasing and Logistics for catalog information. It has already been used by leading German enterprises. BMEcat has been developed to standardize and thus simplify the exchange of product catalogs between vendors and procuring organizations. This project was motivated by the fact that previously, there had been 160 different formats for exchanging product catalogs.

The vendor composes the catalog in electronic form according to the BMEcat standard. This catalog is then transferred to the procuring enterprise as a file. The enterprises integrate the content of the document into the existing catalog. This lets you transfer all of the product data but also lets you update it permanently during the business relationship.

Because BMEcat is based on XML it offers a high level of flexibility and open usability. The decisive success factor is the increasing proliferation of BMEcat in future.

Integrating Transaction Data

To fully benefit from the saving potentials of electronic procurement with SAP SRM you must make use of a seamless electronic communication or transfer of transaction data from purchase orders, payments, and so on to/from vendors and thus avoid typical "paper formats." Several options exist to electronically integrate all vendors, which may have different structures. Table 5.1 lists these options, including their advantages and disadvantages.

Transferring data

Option	Advantages	Disadvantages
Email	Reduced installation and operating costs	No fully automated process flow, inflexible
EDI	Stable data exchange, high integration capability with existing SAP ERP systems	Closed system, high installation and operating costs, inflexible
XML	Flexible, open usability, reduced costs	No standardization
XML-EDI	Flexible, open usability, reduced costs, can be read by humans, predefined tags	No standardization

Table 5.1 Advantages and Disadvantages of Various Data Exchange Formats for Transaction Data

Despite the cost advantages a complete integration of transaction data provides, the solutions that provide the least amount of integration have become widely accepted: fax and email. Unfortunately, you will often find that shopping carts that have been entered and approved in the SAP SRM system (see Section 5.5, Operational Procurement Processing) are printed as purchase orders and faxed to the vendor by the procuring enterprise. The automatic dispatch of an email with purchase order data is frequently considered the highest level of integration.

Usually, you can blame vendors for this unsatisfactory situation because they are not able to integrate transaction data that has been generated in SAP SRM into their backend systems and process it there. However, for procuring enterprises, it is an acceptable solution to automatically dispatch purchase order emails from the SAP SRM system because they can process this procurement transaction without integration gaps. When selecting a vendor, the procuring enterprise that deploys the SAP SRM system should use the integration capability of the vendor as a KO criterion. For example, you should only include products from vendors in the catalog that provide at least email integration.

For all documents that are generated in SAP SRM and exchanged with business partners, the usual exchange formats are supported (see Table 5.2). The following table identifies the selected document types and their usage.

Document type	Print	Fax	Email	XML
Bid invitation	x	x	x	x
Request	x	x	x	x
Auction	x	x	x	x
Contract	x	x	x	x
Purchase order	x	x	x	x
Invoice (for example, evaluated receipt settlement)				x
ERS credit memo (Evaluated Receipt Settlement)	x	x	x	x

Table 5.2 Supported Formats for Documents in SAP SRM

5.3.2   Internal Integration

The *internal integration* of the SAP SRM system, which is also referred to as *backend integration*, is responsible for the smooth processing of procurement transactions in heterogeneous system landscapes without integration gaps. Although SAP SRM provides all essential functions necessary for procurement, you still have to integrate it into existing SAP ERP systems. For example, Financial Accounting is only available in the backend system and critical for complete documentation of all procurement transactions.

SAP SRM provides interfaces that enable integrated use of several SAP ERP systems (release-independent) and further materials management or accounting systems. For the internal integration, you must consider catalog data and transaction data when integrating the SAP SRM system into the backend systems. The type and scope of the integration depend on the degree to which the enterprise uses SAP SRM. In general, if you use more than one system, it is also possible to find the backend system based on the product category. This increases the flexibility of the integration of SAP SRM with the enterprise-internal system landscape considerably. For this purpose, you have to assign the product categories to the relevant target systems in Customizing (see Figure 5.10).

Interfaces in SRM

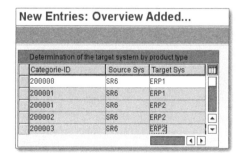

Figure 5.10   Defining the Backend System for the Product Category

For the internal integration of the catalog data, the following question arises: Do you have to mirror items from the catalog into the backend system, for example, the SAP ERP system, as material master records? If so, under which circumstances is redundant data retention necessary? There are no general answers to these questions because they depend

Integration with the backend system

on the individual prerequisites in the enterprises. However, the targeted relocation of the master data management from the MM component of SAP ERP to SAP SRM-MDM makes it more difficult or easier to answer this question. In relation to the quantity of the transaction data that is supposed to be transferred to the backend system, you can consider integration oriented towards accounting and materials management. In both cases, however, the SAP SRM system is still the leading solution for processing catalog procurements.

Standalone operation

When you use *integration induced by accounting*, the standalone operation of SAP SRM, the transaction data is only transferred to the Financial Accounting (FI) component of the SAP ERP system. In this scenario, all activities related to procurement are directly carried out in SAP SRM, and only the accounting-relevant data is transferred to the SAP ERP backend for payment and accounting-related documentation. All procurement process documents, such as purchase order and goods receipt, are directly entered and processed by the SAP SRM system (see Figure 5.11).

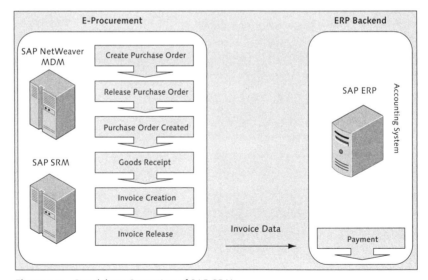

Figure 5.11 Standalone Operation of SAP SRM

This variant is characterized by the lowest level of integration into existing systems, where only the material groups and G/L accounts have to be assigned in the SAP SRM Customizing. This low level of integration leads to system-immanent deficiencies with regard to the documentation of the procurement transactions. For example, the logistical documentation (item, quantity, unit price) takes place in SAP SRM. Through the transfer of integration data (material group, G/L account, values), only the accounting-oriented documentation of the procurement transaction, that is, the consumption, is posted to a G/L account in the SAP ERP system. The documentation's level of detail in the SAP ERP system corresponds to the level of detail of procurements without logistics (see Section 4.2, Procurement Without Logistical Processing).

You can define the appropriate Customizing settings in the SAP SRM system for this scenario using the *Determine backend systems* IMG module. This requires you to define the logical system and the Remote Function Call (RFC) destination. When you activate the Local field (see Figure 5.12), the MM documents such as purchase order, goods receipt, and so on, are created locally in the SAP SRM system.

Fragmentation of the documentation makes it more difficult to comply with or check the compliance with guidelines, and affects procurement controlling. This is because procurement controlling-relevant transaction data is generated in the SAP SRM system and a great number of datasets is directly generated in the MM component of the SAP ERP system by processing standardized procurement transactions that are not suited for e-procurement. That means that two databases with operational procurement data are generated. For effective and efficient procurement controlling, you have to standardize and combine this data. For this purpose, you can use SAP NetWeaver BI as a future-oriented solution (see Chapter 6, Reporting for Procurement Controlling).

Controlling and compliance

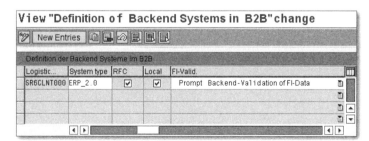

Figure 5.12 Local Creation of MM Documents

When you use *integration induced by MM*, SAP SRM forwards the business processes to the SAP ERP back end, which processes requests, purchase orders, and so on (see Figure 5.13).

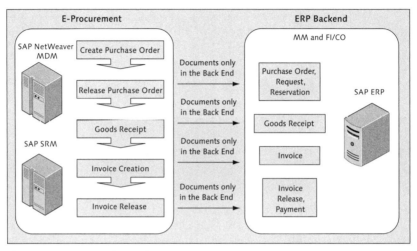

Figure 5.13 Integrated Use of SAP SRM

In this scenario, the integration depth reaches its highest level and thus requires the highest effort in the implementation. When transaction data – for example, of a purchase order – is transferred, the structured data (item number) is transformed in the SAP ERP system into unstructured text items without reference to a material master. Despite the transformation, all documents are automatically generated in the SAP ERP system and can also be processed automatically, if required. The SAP ERP system documents the ordering transactions completely logistically. For procurement controlling, this applies only to material groups that can be evaluated automatically. In the context of controlling, you can evaluate the consumption of, for example, the paper material group in the SAP ERP system. However, here, you cannot differentiate between high-gloss paper, recycling paper, and standard paper.

By defining the transaction types, you also determine the document-oriented functions of the SAP SRM system. The *Define the transaction type* IMG module enables you to define the purchasing documents within a business transaction type that should be used in SAP SRM. In total, there are 16 different transaction object types that determine the business context of a transaction or document type (see Figure 5.14).

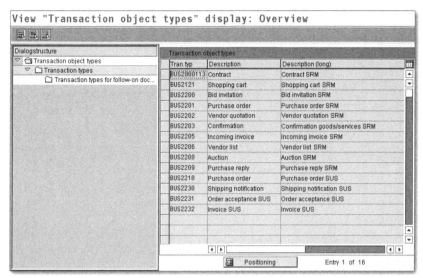

Figure 5.14 Transaction Types in SAP SRM

For each transaction type used in the SAP SRM system, you have to define local and external number range intervals that are used to assign the document numbers during the posting process. Local number range intervals are provided for documents that are directly generated in SAP SRM. The external number range intervals are required to transfer the documents from the SAP SRM system to the integrated SAP ERP backend systems (see Figure 5.15). If there are several integrated backend systems, you have to create separate intervals for each. Please note that there must be the same corresponding number range intervals in the backend systems. In addition, you must activate EXTERNAL for the number assignment because the document numbers are assigned by the SAP SRM system instead of the SAP ERP system.

Number range interval

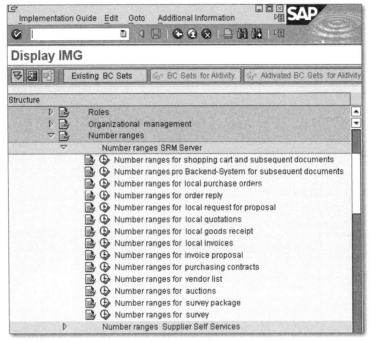

Figure 5.15 Number Ranges

Materials subject
to inventory
management If you use SAP SRM to procure materials that are subject to inventory management, the integration induced by MM and the complete synchronization of the catalog data from the SAP SRM system with the material master data from the SAP ERP system are mandatory. This procedure enables you to access the stock levels of the SAP ERP system from the in-house catalog to define purchase order quantities depending on the stock level. For materials that are not subject to inventory management, you can avoid redundant data retention without affecting the process flow. However, this negatively affects the documentation of the procurement transactions in the SAP ERP system. The transaction data from the SAP SRM system is not transferred to MM in the SAP ERP system on an item basis, but is aggregated at the material group level.

You can also implement the corresponding Customizing settings in the SAP SRM system for the integration induced by MM using the *Determine backend systems* IMG module. In this case, you deactivate the Local field (see Figure 5.16). Then, the MM documents are created in the SAP ERP backend system.

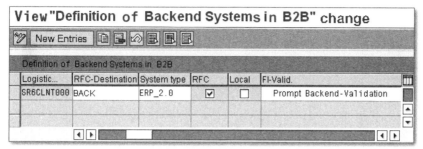

Figure 5.16 Creating MM Documents in the SAP ERP Backend System

In reality, enterprises rarely implement only one of these two integration types. Instead, they are often used together (see Figure 5.17).

Combinations

For example, you can procure standard requirements using SAP SRM with accounting-oriented integration. At the same time, you can use SAP SRM with its user-friendly web interface as a general procurement request tool. Consumers can enter requirements that belong to the material groups that can be ordered via SAP SRM but that cannot be covered with the goods in the catalog as user-defined text items in the shopping cart.

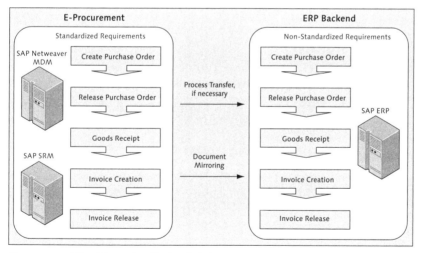

Figure 5.17 Mixed Scenario of Using SAP SRM

This user-friendly purchase requisition (PReq) is transferred to the MM component of the SAP ERP system and, after the vendor has been determined, converted to a purchase order by professional purchasers. Similar to e-procurements, procurement transactions for complex goods that cannot be standardized are directly carried out in the SAP ERP system. The disadvantage of this solution is the partially fragmented documentation of the procurement transactions.

5.3.3 Account Assignment

The business documentation of the procurement transactions requires you to assign the incurring expenses to the corresponding cost settlement objects. The activation of the relevant account assignment objects in the SAP SRM system creates a framework for the assignment of the shopping cart items, and the resulting costs to the cost settlement objects. You activate the existing account assignment objects using the *Define account assignment category* IMG module. This activation depends on the functions used and the offsetting logic implemented in the SAP ERP backend system.

Account assignment objects in SAP SRM

By default, the SAP SRM system provides the following account assignment objects:

▶ **AS (Asset)**
This account assignment category is necessary for procuring goods that must be capitalized.

▶ **CC (Cost Center)**
Account assignments to cost centers are common for the usage of e-procurement.

▶ **OR (Order)**
Internal orders are part of overhead cost controlling and serve to monitor costs for temporary measures.

▶ **FI (Finance and Funds)**
The Public Sector Management (PSM) component enables you to assign accounts directly to the PSM elements commitment item and fund.

▶ **NET (Network)**
Networks are used to control projects logistically. You should activate this account assignment category if the Project Systems (PS) compo-

nent with logistical control is enabled and a direct account assignment from the SAP SRM system to the network transactions is required.

▸ **WBS (WBS element)**
Work breakdown structure elements are part of the PS module and used for commercial controlling (structuring, budgeting, and so on) of complex projects. If the PS module is used and a direct account assignment to the WSP elements is required, you have to select this account assignment category.

▸ **SO (Sales Order)**
The sales order is generated in the Sales & Distribution (SD) component. If the direct account assignment of shopping cart items to sales orders is required, you must use this settlement category.

▸ **STR (Generic Account Assignment)**
You use this account assignment category to define account assignment objects that do not exist in the SAP standard.

To update transaction data from the SAP SRM system to the SAP ERP backend system, you must uniquely assign the account assignment categories of the SAP SRM system to those in the SAP ERP system (see Figure 5.18).

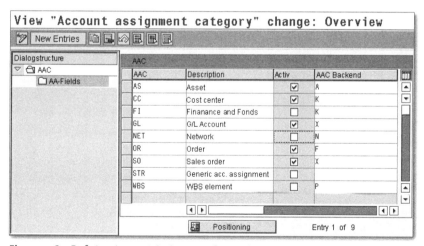

Figure 5.18 Defining Account Assignment Categories

Mapping account
assignment
categories Mapping account assignments in the SAP SRM and ERP systems enables the validation of the account assignment details in the shopping cart items in the SRM system, based on the existing account assignment objects of the ERP system. It also ensures the update quality. Thus, objects that do not exist in the ERP system cannot be transferred.

In addition to mapping the account assignment categories, you must also configure settings with respect to the account determination for a complete integration of the SAP SRM system. This way, the values of incoming invoices and credit memos are updated to the accounts of the general ledger in the SAP ERP system in a technically correct way. G/L accounts are mapped at the product category (product classification) level. At least one account assignment category and one G/L account must be assigned to each product category that is available in the SAP SRM system. Otherwise, the transaction data cannot be updated in the SAP ERP system. If a product category is assigned to several G/L accounts, one combination has to be identified as the default (see Figure 5.19).

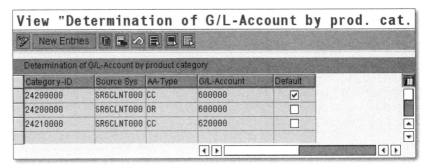

Figure 5.19 Mapping G/L Accounts

When a combination of product category and G/L account is identified as the default, the system proposes the default G/L account as the account assignment for purchasing. The purchaser can ignore the default account assignment and define a different approved exception. The scope for the documentation of procurement transactions is thus restricted to approved exceptions.

5.3.4   Roles

An essential criterion for regulating user activities within an SAP system landscape is the implementation of an authorization concept regarding the use of single roles and composite roles. A role contains transactions for users to assume typical, daily, and periodical tasks. Therefore, the definition of roles is one of the fundamental settings in the SAP SRM system. It should reflect the enterprise's real requirements for the organizational structure regarding strategic and operational purchasing (see Section 3.2, Procurement Organization).

Authorization concept

You determine the roles in the SAP SRM system using Transaction PFCG (Role Maintenance). When designing roles, you assign the transactions or menu tree nodes to the roles. This enables the administrator to have a business view of the processes (tasks). You should consider the auditing requirements and dual-control principle when you design the authorization concept. The technical or system-based implementation of the authorization concept initially comes second. The authorization profiles (collections of authorizations) are automatically generated after the roles have been defined. Because of the assigned transactions, the corresponding authorizations are usually set automatically. You then have to customize the details of the authorization profile you created, in accordance with the requirements of the authorization concept. You do so by defining the characteristics for the authorization objects, such as purchasing groups.

Role maintenance

Role definition usually distinguishes between single roles and composite roles.

Depending on the structure and details of the authorization concept, single roles consist of specific transactions and authorizations that are needed to use or process a functional area. In total, 28 single roles are available (see Figure 5.20). The number of roles indirectly reflects the scope of functions of the SAP SRM system.

Single roles

In this context, the SAP reference user roles should be considered as templates and a way to orient yourself. The idea to use only SAP reference roles to structure the role and authorization concept sounds very tempting. However, in reality, the requirements for the authorization concept are much more complex than in the standard because it depends on the flows of the business processes and task management in the enterprise. It therefore makes sense to customize the reference roles. In this case, you should copy or derive enterprise-specific roles from the reference concept and then adapt them to the requirements of the enterprise.

Figure 5.20 Default Single Roles in the SAP SRM System

The range of functions of single roles or the scope of the transactions that are available in a role depends on the application area. For better handling, less complex roles are preferred in day-to-day business. This corresponds to the concept of "minimum authorizations," that is, to implement authorizations as "strict" as necessary (see Figure 5.21).

Composite roles   Composite roles serve as a pool for single roles. A composite role lets you combine several single roles, which lets you better structure single roles. By default, SAP SRM provides 25 composite roles (see Figure 5.22).

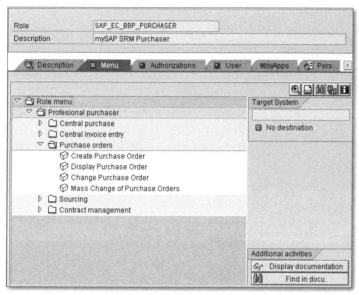

Figure 5.21 Scope of Functions of the "mySAP SRM Purchaser" Role

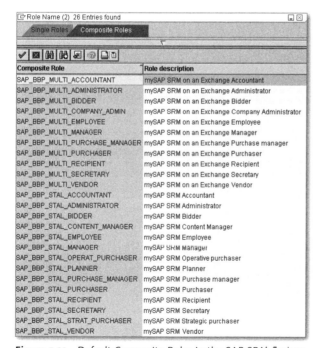

Figure 5.22 Default Composite Roles in the SAP SRM System

Composite roles are typically used by persons who work with several applications of the SAP SRM system, for example, using strategic and operational purchasing at the same time. This applies mostly to small and medium-sized businesses (SMB), where the specialization is below average. The MYSAP SRM OPERATIVE PURCHASER composite role, for example, contains the SAP SRM: EMPLOYEE and SAP SRM: OPERATIVE PURCHASER single roles by default (see Figure 5.23).

Documentation Designing a role is not a one-time event, but a continuous process. Due to release changes and changing conditions, guidelines, or legal regulations (for example, data protection laws, Sarbancs-Oxley Act, and so on), you have to adjust the authorization concept to the new circumstances. End-to-end documentation should be the prerequisite for the authorization concept.

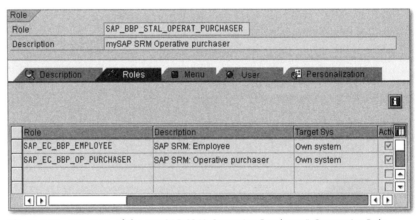

Figure 5.23 Structure of the "mySAP SRM Operative Purchaser" Composite Role

5.4   Strategic Procurement Management

Decentralization of the purchasing management The strict separation of strategic and operational tasks when using SAP SRM allows for a complete decentralization of the purchasing management, as well as for centralization of strategic tasks (see Figure 5.24).

For procurements, this is a symbiotic combination that hasn't been available in this form before. You can benefit from the advantages of both the centralization (homogenization, utilization of synergy effects) and the decentralization (reduction of the processing time and costs). Despite decentralized purchasing management, you can achieve a high level of standardization and homogenization for procurement. This way, you can avoid the heterogenization of the processes and procured goods that usually results from decentralization (see Figure 5.25).

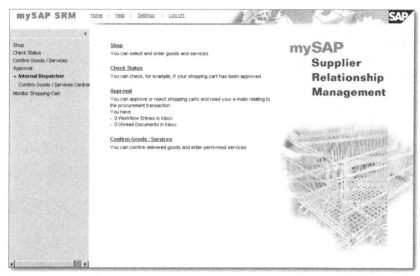

Figure 5.24 Initial Screen in SAP SRM1

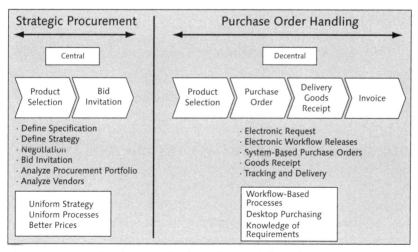

Figure 5.25 Central and Decentralized Distribution of the Tasks

Strategic purchasing tasks

Strategic tasks are found primarily during the phase when purchase orders are initiated and consist of market surveys, vendor selection, initiation of business contacts, bid invitation negotiations, and so on. These are unstructured tasks that are centrally assumed by the strategic purchasing department in the enterprise and completed by adding items to the in-house catalog. The advantage of this solution is that you have to perform these time- and thus cost-intensive activities only once and not for every procurement transaction.

Reporting functions

For system-based support of strategic procurement tasks, SAP SRM provides reporting functions. These include the spend analysis to analyze vendor relationships, output volumes, and so on, and category management to plan the goods that should be added to the catalog, as well as pricing, or sales promotions that specifically address the consumer. These reporting functions you precisely control consumption. Furthermore, the entire bid invitation process is electronically supported by *e-tendering* or *e-requests* (see Figure 5.26).

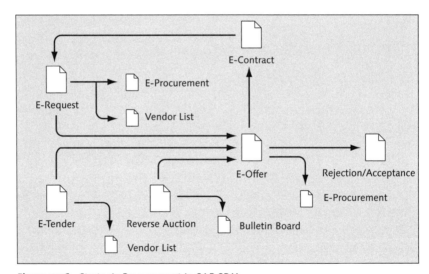

Figure 5.26 Strategic Procurement in SAP SRM

SAP SRM supports you in carrying out public and non-public bid invitations. The major difference between the two is the type of publication of the existing material and service requirement for potential vendors.

Non-public bid invitations use e-requests and address only selected vendors. Known bidders, or those who have been identified through preselection are asked via email to submit a binding bid. Access data to the SAP SRM system is also sent via email, which enables potential vendors to enter their bid directly into the SAP SRM system. To do this, user master records must be available in the system for the selected bidders. After the bids have been received, they are analyzed and then accepted or rejected.

Bid invitation in the private business sector

For e-tendering, potential bidders are publicly asked to submit their bids, for example, with publications on dedicated portals. After a bidder has indicated interest, he receives access data and can then enter a bid in the SAP SRM system. Bids are checked after the opening date has been reached. The order is placed with the vendor who submitted the best bid. Before placing the order, you can also convert the bid invitation to a *reverse auction* (see Figure 5.26). By converting the bid invitation to a live reverse auction (similar to eBay auctions), all bidders involved are asked to check their bid during a certain period of time and underbid the lowest price. With this innovation, the strategic purchasing department indirectly gains leeway for price negotiations with vendors.

Bid invitations in the public sector

Bid invitations and requests are based on service specifications that uniquely define the existing requirements. In SAP SRM, you can generate these service specifications by creating bid invitations and requests as follows:

Service specifications

▶ The requirements are manually specified on the basis of the strategic purchaser's decisions.

▶ The requirements are manually specified on the basis of a requirement request that has been entered in the SAP SRM system by selecting the relevant items (see Section 5.5, Operational Procurement Processing).

▶ Bid invitations and requests are automatically derived from the service specifications of existing contracts.

▶ By grouping existing requirement requests, the service specifications and thus bid invitations and requests are automatically created in the SAP SRM system.

Vendor contracts

Vendor contracts are the result of bid invitations or reverse auctions that have been carried out with system support. They can be implemented in the system either by transferring the advertised products to the in-house catalog (see Appendix A, Process 1a: Structure and Maintenance of the E-Catalog (Push Strategy)) or by creating outline agreements in the SAP SRM or SAP ERP system (see Appendix A, Process 1b: Structure and Maintenance of Outline Agreements in the SAP System (Push Strategy)).

Bid Invitations in the Public Administration

The functions of the SAP SRM systems for carrying out bid invitations focus mainly on the requirements of enterprises operating in the private sector. For ordering parties in the public sector, the scope of functions is not sufficient because there are numerous legal regulations that must be complied with when carrying out bid invitations in the public sector.

Award of contract regulations in the public sector

The public ordering party has to comply with the corresponding award of contract regulations when placing the order. This includes, for example, the Act against Restraint of Competition, Regulation on the Award of Public Contracts, Budget Order as well as the Conditions concerning Contracts for Supplies and Services, General Conditions of Contract for the Execution of Building Works, and Conditions concerning Contracts for Freelance Supplies and Services. When procuring the goods and services listed in the electronic procurement catalog (e-catalog) you need to develop, you must comply with these regulations. This means that you have to issue invitations to bid for all items individually using awards of contracts for a specific period of time and quantity. Consequently, the e-catalog may not include goods and services for which no corresponding award of contract process has been carried out.

Public procurement law in e-procurement

The applicable public procurement law restricts the use of e-procurement in public administration considerably because you can only add items to the e-catalog when the bid invitations have been carried out in compliance with the public procurement law. The fast pace of product cycles and the high level of price variability, however, require shorter procurement cycles. This places high requirements on the central strategic procurement management, and makes it necessary to react flexibly to changing market conditions. To ensure that invitations to bid in the public sector are issued according to compliance and supported by the system, you must use additional solutions that comply with the public procurement law.

5.5 Operational Procurement Processing

Operational procurements in SAP SRM enable an efficient, system-based support of activities, such as the entry of *procurement requests, purchase orders, and goods or invoice receipts* (see Figure 5.27).

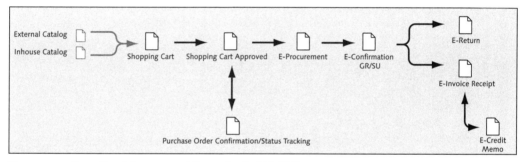

Figure 5.27 Operational Procurement Processing in SAP SRM

5.5.1 Purchase Order

A purchaser needs only basic software equipment, that is, access to the Internet or intranet and a web browser. Operational purchasing management in SAP SRM can thus be summarized as "purchasing per mouse click." It starts with selecting the item that is appropriate for the existing requirement from the catalog and composing the shopping cart (see Figure 5.28). This procedure is supported by powerful and comprehensive search helps (see Section 5.2.2, Using Catalog Data).

Purchasing per mouse click

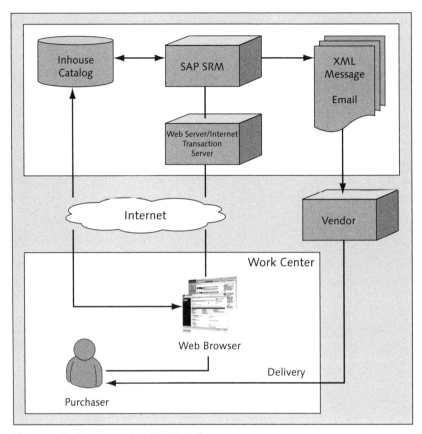

Figure 5.28 Procurement at the Workplace

Favorites As an alternative, you can limit the view of the catalog content using favorites. This minimizes the search effort for recurring requirements (see Figure 5.29). Any user who has ordered something at *Amazon.com* should be familiar with this procedure.

User interface In this context, the benefits of a user-friendly front end that is still technically complex enough for the various tasks become obvious. SAP SRM's user-friendly web interface enables employees to enter requirement requests or purchase orders by specifying the content of their shopping cart. Unlike in the SAP ERP system, time-consuming and complex data entries into the purchase order form are unnecessary here. Consequently, you don't require dedicated knowledge to use SAP SRM, which promotes a quick and wide acceptance in the enterprise.

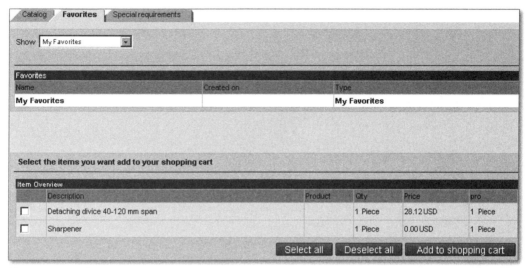

Figure 5.29 Ordering Transaction in SAP SRM

Thanks to its user-friendliness, almost every consumer in the enterprise can use SAP SRM and directly specify his requirements by selecting the items available in the catalog or by entering requests with user-defined text. In many enterprises, SAP SRM is also used as a general data entry system for procurement requests.

Easy usage

This enables you to substitute PReqs in SAP ERP. These are mainly used by manufacturing enterprises to procure direct goods. In the service sector, and for sales-oriented enterprises, the PReqs from the SAP ERP system have been rarely accepted because of functional deficits for combining several PReqs in one purchase order, or because of their high level of data entry effort.

Purchase requisitions in SAP ERP

Purchasing management in SAP SRM involves three steps: Select goods/ services → Add goods/services to shopping cart → Complete and confirm shopping cart (see Figure 5.30).

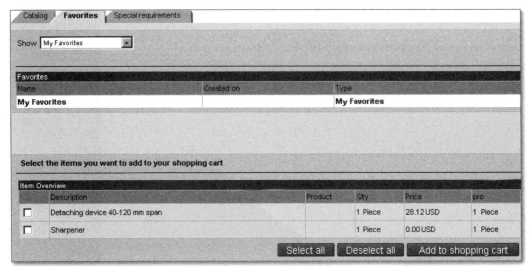

Figure 5.30 Initial Screen in the E-Procurement Application of SAP SRM

Selecting the goods

You can select the goods via reference to old purchase orders or templates by clicking on the OLD PURCHASE ORDERS AND TEMPLATES hyperlink (see Figure 5.31). In this case, the purchaser can search for the appropriate purchase order in a specific period of time by describing items or using the name of the shopping cart (see Figure 5.31).

Figure 5.31 Selecting the Goods from Existing Purchase Orders

By copying and adjusting the existing documents to the given requirements, you can generate new purchase orders quickly and efficiently. Then, the purchase order data (prices, minimum purchase order quantity, and so on) is verified in the product catalog (see Section 5.2.1, Creating and Maintaining Catalog Data). This procedure is especially suited for procuring recurring requirements.

You can also identify the required product by searching the catalog. For this purpose, you start the catalog management system using the OLD PURCHASE ORDERS AND TEMPLATES hyperlink (see Figure 5.31). The catalog enables the purchaser to use various search options, such as searching by hierarchical classification according to eClass, by product index, by vendor category, and so on. You can select the goods and services by entering the quantity in the QUANTITY field. When the entered quantity is below the minimum purchase order quantity, the system displays an exception message. In this case, the shopping cart cannot be saved (see Figure 5.32).

Searching the catalog

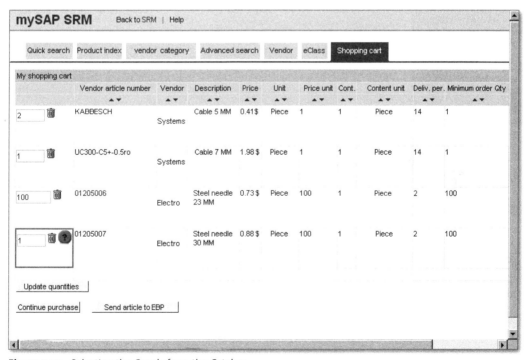

Figure 5.32 Selecting the Goods from the Catalog

Here, the benefits of e-procurement or externalization of the catalog data maintenance (see Section 5.2.1, Creating and Maintaining Catalog Data) become obvious. Vendors are responsible for the semantic correctness of the maintained catalog data. Technically and formally correct purchase orders are the result. Complex renegotiations or clarification processes can be entirely avoided.

Procuring Assets

The procurement of products in the SAP SRM system that must be capitalized represents a special case because of their complex integration with the SAP ERP system. As already described in Section 5.2.1, Creating and Maintaining Catalog Data, you must identify products that must be capitalized as such in the context of catalog management.

Requirements of assets procurement
This classification ensures that account assignments to assets are mandatory for ordering goods that must be capitalized. Usually, a user with professional knowledge of asset accounting should be involved in the approval workflow when you procure assets. This requirement is based on the complex functions in the asset subsidiary ledger, on the one hand, and on the currently insufficient integration of SAP SRM with the asset subsidiary ledger of the SAP ERP system, on the other hand.

Asset master records
The procurement of new products that must be capitalized generally requires asset master records in the SAP ERP system. It doesn't matter whether the procurement in SAP SRM is triggered by a catalog selection or conventionally in the SAP ERP system. Currently, you cannot define asset master records in SAP SRM and thus must use SAP ERP for this purpose. To define master records in SAP ERP, you require sound system and technical knowledge because numerous controlling specifications need to be made, for example, regarding the depreciation areas, depreciation keys, inventory number, and so on (see Figure 5.33).

The technical and functional complexity illustrates that only professional users – and not all common requesters in the enterprise – should create asset master records in the SAP ERP system.

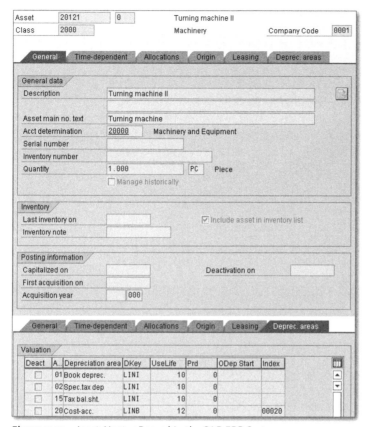

Figure 5.33 Asset Master Record in the SAP ERP System

You can procure assets in the SAP SRM or SAP ERP system in a technically correct way only with the help of an asset accountant. When you
procure new assets without any master record existing in the SAP ERP
system, the asset accountant must work with two systems. The requisitioner enters the procurement request in the SAP SRM system. Because
the assets must be capitalized, the asset accountant needs to approve
them. You can convert the requirement request to a purchase order after
the account assignment to an asset master record that exists in SAP ERP.
For this purpose, the asset accountant must change the system and create
an appropriate master record with the corresponding controlling parameters in SAP ERP, using Transaction AS01 (Create Asset Master Record).
Then, he must change from the SAP ERP system to the SAP SRM system
again to carry out the account assignment to the asset. This complex

Involvement of the
asset accountant

and user-unfriendly workaround closes the functional gap in the SAP SRM system and needs to be used when assets are procured for the first time.

Procurement request

Using SAP SRM as a general procurement request tool ensures that the information management requirement for entering data at their location of origin is implemented in a cost-efficient way. Many requirements emerge decentralized in the enterprise, in departments, warehouses, and so on. To request these requirements by using SAP SRM, you only need a web browser. The ability to compose the shopping cart in a user-friendly way, either by using a reference to existing documents or directly searching the catalog, contributes considerably to the acceptance of SAP SRM in enterprises. A shopping cart that has been filled using these options (see Figure 5.34), however, may have to be completed or approved before it can be converted to a legally binding purchase order.

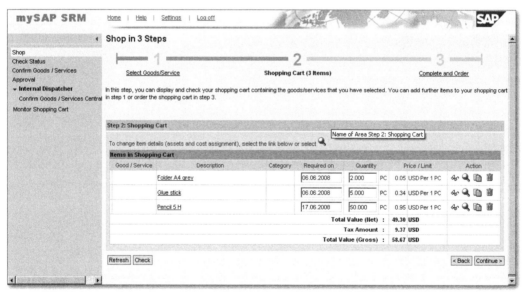

Figure 5.34 Shopping Cart in SAP SRM

Approval procedures

The definition of approval procedures lets you structure the procurement process flow for procurement requests. In general, you can distinguish between purchase requisitions that do not require approval and purchase requisitions that do require approval. The first variant is based on the sole responsibility of the person who requests the procurement. The procurement request is accepted by the purchasing department through login and/or password entry, or similar procedures. The purchase order of the consumer triggers the goods delivery without further checks. Data that has been obtained through monitoring allows for subsequent checks. Although the permitted items are already limited by providing the goods catalog, and although selected checks such as budgetary control can be carried out automatically, procurement requests or purchase orders that do not require an approval are rarely used in day-to-day business.

For purchase orders that require approval, enterprise-specific approval procedures form the basis for the coordination and control of procurements. In the context of system-based approvals, each shopping cart (requests with user-defined text and catalog purchase orders) is automatically forwarded to the responsible instances and must be approved by those (see Figure 5.35).

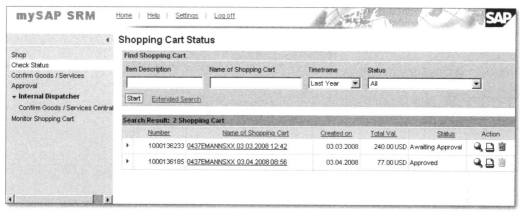

Figure 5.35 Status of the Shopping Carts

The responsible persons are stored in the SAP SRM organizational management, and the approval path (responsibility according to purchase order amount and product category) is set. For this purpose, you can use the NOTICE RECEIVER IMG module in Customizing. The appropriate role is assigned to the application scenario, for example, SHOPPING CART APPROVAL (see Figure 5.36). This way you define which users receive which workflow notices for which application scenarios, according to their position.

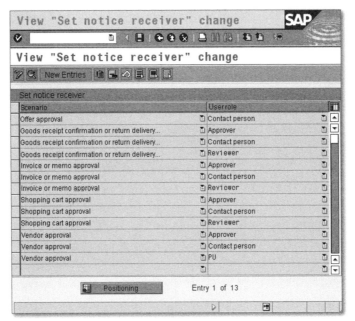

Figure 5.36 Setting the Workflow Notices

Dangerous goods

If the catalog contains dangerous goods or goods that must be capitalized, it makes sense to implement an approval procedure that is based on product categories. If you use approval procedures that are based on purchase order amounts, you should develop and implement unified regulations during the implementation phase of SAP SRM as early as possible to minimize the required effort.

Completion and Approval Workflows

In SAP SRM, you can define completion and approval workflows for various business objects, such as shopping carts, purchase orders, contracts, bid invitations, and so on. Completion workflows can be regarded as a preliminary stage of the approval. The responsible persons are informed, for example, of the created shopping carts and prompted to add missing information, such as the account assignment to a specific cost center. This ensures a semantic quality of the documentation of procurement transactions and at the same time decentralizes the entry activity significantly. Completion workflows enable employees to create shopping carts without knowledge of account assignments.

You configure the starting conditions in the application component of the SAP SRM system using Transaction SWB_PROCUREMENT (Maintain B2B Starting conditions).

Configuring the starting conditions

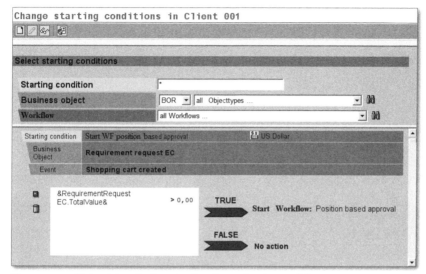

Figure 5.37 Maintaining the Starting Conditions for the Workflow

Figure 5.37 illustrates the starting condition for the position-based approval. In this case, the approval workflow is started when the total value of the requirement request or the created shopping cart exceeds 0.00 US dollar. That means you defined a zero tolerance limit. All shopping carts need to be approved before they can be converted to legally binding purchase orders. You can configure the conditions individually using several nested conditions. For example, you can define that the start of the approval workflow doesn't depend on the shopping cart but on the value of the most expensive shopping cart item (see Figure 5.38).

As a general rule, you can say that SAP SRM provides comprehensive design options for completion and approval workflows. Despite this wide range of variants, real-life projects should start with a reduced number of workflow variants, which should be successively adapted to the requirements of the enterprise.

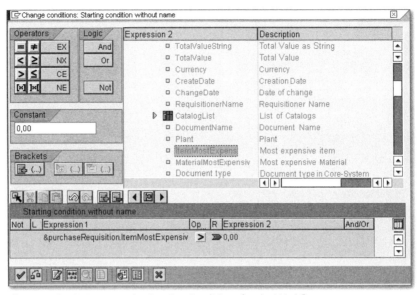

Figure 5.38 Maintaining the Starting Conditions for the Workflow

Shopping carts containing items with user-defined text

Shopping carts that contain items with user-defined text represent a special case for purchase orders that require approval. These are requests that cannot be covered with the standard selection of the goods catalog and must be procured conventionally via MM in the SAP ERP system (see Section 4.2, Procurement without Logistical Processing). For strategic purchasing, the number of requests with user-defined text is a good indicator of the extent to which the goods on offer in the catalog are compatible with the requirements in the enterprise. If there are too many items with user-defined text, you should carry out an analysis to add items to the catalog, if required.

The approval of a shopping cart leads to purchase orders or purchase requisitions (for items that are not listed in the catalog) in SAP SRM, which are transferred to the SAP ERP system. You can transfer the purchase order to the vendor electronically either as an XML purchase order via the Business Connector or as an email with purchase order data in PDF format. The method for transferring the purchase order depends considerably on your integration options (see Section 5.3.1, External Integration).

Approval with Duet

The software product *Duet*, which has been developed in close col-laboration of SAP and Microsoft, allows for a particularly user-friendly approval procedure.

SAP and Microsoft

It enables you to access selected SAP ERP or SAP SRM functions directly from Microsoft Outlook. The approver, for example, can participate in purchasing management without having to log on to the SAP SRM sys-tem every time. The shopping carts that must be approved are sent via email to the authorized approver's Outlook inbox, including header and item data of the shopping cart. The Duet functions in Outlook enable him to reject or accept the purchase requisition. The transaction data in the SAP SRM system are automatically updated, and the resulting pur-chase order is automatically generated. The provision of selected SAP SRM functions in Outlook contributes significantly to the acceptance by superiors. Moreover, lead times are reduced due to shorter approval times because superiors are informed about the procurement request to be approved almost in real time and not when they log on to the SAP SRM system the next time.

Purchase order via Outlook

In addition to operational functions, Duet also delivers reporting func-tions, including reports in Outlook. This enables superiors to be informed about the aggregated procurement volume, available budgets, or ABC analyses, for example, without having to deal with reporting tools. These reports simplify the approval process considerably because all decision-relevant data is directly provided.

5.5.2   Goods Receipt

As already mentioned, procurement in SAP SRM supports a complete decentralization of operational procurement activities. Consequently, the goods receipt is directly confirmed by the consumer. The technical invoice verification is integrated in the check of the delivered goods and comparison with the underlying purchase order information to com-ply with the commercial obligation to give notice of defects. For items that must be capitalized, the goods receipt defines the capitalization date (capitalization date = goods receipt date).

Confirmation of goods receipt

Decentralized goods receipt

The dual-control principle may be a problem for the decentralized goods receipt because the requisitioner and the goods receiving clerk are the same person. To be able to adhere to the dual-control principle, you must avoid that the same person has both responsibilities. This is not always possible in day-to-day business and leads to additional costs (such as license and training costs).

Alternatively, you can reduce the process costs by using a subsequent dual-control principle. That is, during procurement controlling, you could subsequently check who initiated the procurement transaction and which changes have been made to the purchase order and goods receipt.

5.5.3 Entering Invoices

Due to the standardized processing of all procurement transactions in SAP SRM, common invoice entries with reference (see Section 4.2.3, Consequences for Procurements Without Logistics in FI) become obsolete.

Evaluated receipt settlement

Instead of the known logistical invoice verification, you can use the automatic *ERS* (*Evaluated Receipt Settlement*). For standardized items with a high order frequency, vendors participate in this procedure because they can also save process costs. For the automatic ERS, the goods quantity that has been confirmed for goods receipt is multiplied by the respective prices from the purchase order. Considering the agreed upon payment conditions, the invoice amount that has to be paid (also referred to as credit for the vendor) is determined and transferred to the SAP ERP system where it is processed, affecting payment.

Credit memo

The credit memo, that is, the information on the amount that must be paid, can be made available for the vendor in the same way as a purchase order (XML credit memo, or email with PDF attachment). It can be transferred case-related or periodically as a collective credit memo.

Entering invoices manually

As an alternative to the automatic evaluated receipt settlement, you can enter invoices manually in the SAP SRM system with reference to the purchase order. However, you should only use this option if the vendor doesn't accept the ERS procedure.

5.6 Prerequisites for Procurement Processing with SAP SRM

In literature, e-procurement has been praised as the all-in-one solution suitable for every purpose in its initial phase. The initial euphoria was quickly followed by disillusionment. The following restrictions eliminate the potential for reduced processing times and costs:

Cost/benefit analysis

▸ SAP SRM leads to additional costs for software and hardware.

▸ Common master data management is replaced by Content Management of the goods catalog.

▸ Despite additional costs and effort, e-procurement can only partially cover the enterprise requirements. The procurement functions of the SAP ERP system must be operated in parallel in the enterprise.

E-procurement cannot present a comprehensive solution concept for all procurement areas. Consequently, you should take these restrictions into account before implementing SAP SRM and first carry out basic vendor and requirements analyses. The vendor analysis should reveal whether vendors are able to participate in e-procurement and provide their products in the form of a catalog file.

The requirements analysis should clarify whether the order frequency of the e-procurement items justifies the use of SAP SRM. In literature, when goods are analyzed with regard to their suitability for e-procurement, a distinction is often made between direct and indirect goods. *Direct goods* are procured for manufacturing purposes and are integrated into finished products. *Indirect goods* are low-value items, such as office supplies, spare parts, auxiliary material, and expendables. They are also referred to as *MRO goods* (Maintenance, Repair and Operations). Direct goods are considered to be viable for e-procurement because their procurement can be planned, and because of a high level of standardization.

Requirements analysis

Distinguishing between direct and indirect goods is obsolete because this would mean that e-procurement solutions are not suited for non-manufacturing enterprises. You should use the classification scheme shown in Figure 5.39 to analyze which products should be procured electronically and which should be procured conventionally.

Classification of goods

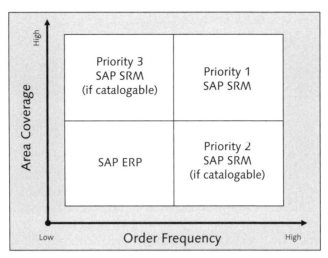

Figure 5.39 Classification of the Procurement Processes for E-Procurement

Reducing the
process costs

The goal of e-procurement is reducing the procurement process costs by minimizing search and initiation activities, and reducing the follow-up costs by homogenizing the requirement coverage in the enterprise. For goods with a high order frequency, you can reduce process costs the most because the search and initiation activities are minimized considerably by providing a goods catalog that complies with general guidelines. For decentralized emerging requirements, you can take advantage of additional savings potentials if these requirements can be covered by standardized and interchangeable goods. This means that goods that are used in the enterprise can be interchanged, which reduces the follow-up costs because no specialized usage and maintenance knowledge is required.

Profitability
analysis

Therefore, to check the e-procurement capability of goods, you should use the dimensions order frequency, area coverage, and ability of goods to be entered into a catalog. In the context of the subsequent profitability analysis, you should determine whether the number of e-procurement-capable procurement transactions is sufficient to compensate for the operating costs of the catalog management software and the SAP SRM system by saving process and procurement costs.

6 Reporting for Procurement Controlling

Data that has been recorded within procurement processing must be processed with suitable reporting to achieve the goals of procurement controlling. This chapter first provides an overview of the reports that have been created in the MM and Financial Accounting (FI) components, and which are included in the framework of standard reporting in the SAP system. To determine the usage rate of Materials Management you also require reports that contain procurement data of both components. This makes individual reports necessary because standard reporting doesn't cover this requirement. The chapter describes the implementation options based on a sample report in the SAP ERP system as well as in SAP NetWeaver Business Intelligence (SAP NetWeaver BI).

6.1 Objectives of Procurement Controlling

Production and retail enterprises, but also public administrations, must increasingly ensure to reduce the costs for the production of goods or the purchase of consumption goods. This is closely linked to procurement processes, which must sustainably and continuously be improved. In theory and practice, there are different controlling instruments you can provide to the respective decision makers within *procurement controlling* (also referred to as *purchasing controlling*).

Procurement controlling is a part of operational controlling. It is used to enable the planning, control, and supply of information for the provision of production factors for the operational production process.

Definition of procurement controlling

Procurement controlling enables you to make the following decisions and definitions:

- In-house production or external procurement
- Determination of lower and upper price limits
- Optimal order quantity
- ABC analyses

Through procurement controlling purchasers receive information that is relevant for their purchasing decision. The controller must ensure that purchasers are provided with the corresponding cost and business volume magnitudes from operational Financial Accounting (FI). Based on this information you can, for example, determine the upper price limit of the goods to be procured, and make decisions with regard to in-house or external production.

Where is procurement-controlling implemented? From an organizational perspective, procurement controlling can be implemented both by a central unit (e.g., central procurement department) and decentralized departments with appropriate "procurement competencies" and authority to make decisions.

In both application scenarios, procurement controlling must be integrated into the enterprise's organization in such a way that access to the relevant information is ensured at all times. Only then can effective and controlled reporting be ensured. This enterprise-internal information is supplemented by data from external enterprises (vendors) that is relevant for the procurement process. This lets you take advantage of the improvement potential both on the vendor and enterprise side.

In procurement controlling, you should consider all procurement processes of an enterprise that contain raw materials, commodities, services, and assets. The goal is to achieve more efficient procurement processes, which can have monetary effects (cost savings) and nonmonetary effects (reduction of lead times).

An essential prerequisite to achieving these objectives is to ensure smooth communication and cooperation with vendors.

Providing information Another task of procurement controlling is to provide information about the enterprise's internal and external processes. Moreover, evaluation criteria (e.g., procurement costs and quality standards) must be defined for objective evaluations.

Information must be provided in suitable reports. The following sections describe possible report types in general, and explain the requirements of reporting – including the required report components.

6.2 Report Types

In general, you distinguish among the following types of reports:

▶ Standard or planned reports

▶ Triggered or variance reports (exception reporting)

▶ Individually requested or requirements reports (ad-hoc reports)

These also exist in the SAP system.

Examples for standard reports are debtor and creditor standard reports, which analyze open items, when these are due, and the currency risk contained in them. These reports are created on a regular basis, and in batch mode, because they put a heavy load on system resources. Executing these reports in dialog mode would not be reasonable. They are then provided to the user.

Standard reports

In the SAP system, *exception reporting* enables you to highlight objects in drilldown reports in color if values exceed or fall below certain tolerance limits.

Exception reporting

Most reports in the SAP system are individually requested reports, that is, when information is required, the user executes the corresponding report.

Requirements reports

Requirements reports should not be confused with ad-hoc reports, for which the user does not define the information that is supposed to be provided until report execution. For all reports previously mentioned, the information is output prior to execution.

Ad-hoc reports

Reporting should provide decision-relevant information to a specific recipient group. You should ensure user-friendly presentation of the data, that is, you should consider the report recipient's previous knowl-

Reporting requirements

edge. A reporting tree hierarchy – as it is requested for management information systems – offers clear information presentation and should be configured for every recipient individually.

The information submitted must be true, objectively verifiable, and up-to-date as much as possible, so that the user doesn't lose confidence in the reporting system or make decisions based on outdated data. Reports should be provided to the recipient at regular intervals, and indicate the objectives achieved in the past as well as the future prospects of the enterprise. The information content can be increased considerably by delivering comparison objects. Individual information and totals should be clearly separated from each other, and exceptional situations will be quickly recognizable, for example, through *color coding*. To facilitate the recording and storing of information for the recipient, it should be possible to receive information graphically formatted, so that it is easier to remember.

External information The integration of external information represents another requirement. The reports that should be examined usually provide information that was created within the enterprise, or they obtain external information that is required for enterprise-internal operational tasks. Two interfaces are available for external information that is primarily used to support decision-making; however, these are not supported in standard reports. By connecting external service providers, which is also a requirement for report systems, you can add information to the information system of the enterprise to subsequently forward to employees. According to Reichmann, this is also referred to as an "information broker," whose information can be added to the SAP system via interfaces. Therefore, you must ensure a flexible and dynamic report system design. This enables you to respond to internal requirements changes and adapt to changes in external conditions.

In concrete terms, this means that newly defined reports can be readily added to reporting, old reports can be removed, and interfaces exist or can be created for new connections.

Weaknesses of traditional reporting Traditional reporting has the following weaknesses:

- ▶ Lack of qualified information, glut of unqualified information
- ▶ Outdated information

- No query options
- Non-specific information

These weaknesses can be eliminated with a dialog-oriented information system, through queries at the touch of a button, and a demand-based information frequency. In SAP reports, at least on the system side, you can avoid time delays during information forwarding because this standard software is a real time information system. Through interactive reporting with drilldown and drillup functionality, users can question certain facts even if no person responsible is available. This is particularly crucial for users who are less interested in detailed information and consequently receive highly aggregated information, which results in a loss of information. The SAP system provides the technical options to resolve the weaknesses just described.

In the Materials Management (MM) and Financial Accounting (FI) components, the SAP system provides various standard reports, which are described in the following sections.

6.3 Standard Reporting

Reporting can have different concepts. Depending on the report trigger, a distinction is made between *system-active*, *user-active*, and *dialog systems*.

In system-active reporting, the activity originates from the report system, in other words, the report is automatically generated by the system (for example, depreciation postings). Here, you need to differentiate between inflexible and flexible systems, depending on the change option of the report system. If the activity originates from the user, this system is referred to as a user-active system. In this system, the user triggers the data selection through requests. Dialog systems provide the highest performance. Here, man machine communication takes places to satisfy specific information requirements. In addition to basic queries, dialog systems also provide decision and forecast models.

System-active vs. user-active reporting

6.3.1 Evaluations in General Ledger Accounting

General Ledger Accounting is the primary data basis of the financial information system. As the central processing group, it aggregates all value data of an enterprise. The financial information system's goal is to evaluate this large amount of base data in dialog mode and display information in manageable units on the screen.

G/L account
information system

G/L account transaction numbers are the primary source of this base data for the G/L account information system in general ledger accounting. This lets you analyze the relevant G/L accounts for MM, in other words, the accounts to which you can post via purchase orders from MM. Alternatively, you can make a direct assignment to these G/L accounts via a vendor invoice (see Section 4.2.1, Entering Vendor Invoices in Financial Accounting [FI]).

Evaluation is restricted to the value-based presentation of procurements that are relevant from the point of view of Financial Accounting (FI). A quantity-based analysis of the procurement process is not possible.

Typical evaluation
reports

The following list describes typical evaluation reports in general ledger accounting:

▸ **G/L account balances**
The G/L account balance list shows the following numbers, delimited by months: balance carryforward at the beginning of the fiscal year, total of the carryforward period, debit of the reporting period, credit total of the reporting period, and accumulated balance of the reporting period.

CoCd	G/L acct	Short Text	Crcy	BusA	Balance Carryforward	Balance,prev.periods	Debit rept.period	Credit report.per.	Accumulated balance
0001	310020	MB/td.gds	USD		252,309.75	0.00	3,562,020.00	2,339,059.80	1,475,269.95
0001	310030	CB/td.gds.	USD		1,024,447.60	0.00	6,605,472.50	2,977,070.80	4,652,849.30
0001	310040	TB./td.gds.	USD		1,462,692.93	0.00	16,855,246.30	9,673,503.39	8,644,435.84
0001	310050	Acc./td.gds.	USD		168,748.28	0.00	1,088,292.60	837,387.31	419,653.57
0001	400020	Raw mats consumption	USD		0.00	0.00	15,827,021.30	0.00	15,827,021.30
0001	420000	Direct labor costs	USD		0.00	0.00	156,527.31	190.20	156,337.11
0001	422000	Downtime pay	USD		0.00	0.00	2,794.81	0.00	2,794.81
0001	430000	Salaries	USD		0.00	0.00	1,019,968.95	0.00	1,019,968.95
0001	432000	Continued pay	USD		0.00	0.00	49,289.13	0.00	49,289.13
0001	440000	Social security	USD		0.00	0.00	32,292.86	39.56	32,253.30
0001	440100	Soc. secur., salary	USD		0.00	0.00	218,973.22	0.00	218,973.22
0001	449000	Other personnel exp.	USD		0.00	0.00	12,840.00	0.00	12,840.00
0001	470000	Occupancy costs	USD		0.00	0.00	2,021.55	0.00	2,021.55
0001	477001	Trade Shows, Seminar	USD		0.00	0.00	4,862.07	0.00	4,862.07
0001	481000	Est. depreciation	USD		0.00	0.00	143,532.00	0.00	143,532.00
0001	483000	Estimated interest	USD		0.00	0.00	18,862.00	0.00	18,862.00
0001	790000	Unfinished products	USD		1,151,833.58	0.00	7,127,029.97	7,910,174.46	368,689.09

Figure 6.1 Standard SAP Report "G/L Account Balances"

▶ **Line item evaluation**

This report creates a list of all open or cleared items that you can delimit by time. The list contains G/L account items that are open at the indicated key date, as well as cleared items whose clearing dates are displayed in the defined selection area. You can select all accounts or only those that contain open items. In addition to the usual item information, you are also provided with the following account assignments, if they are contained in the item: cost center and plant, project number, and order number.

Posted on	Type	DocumentNo	Doc. Date	PK	NP	Assignment	Clearing	Clrng doc	Crcy	Amount in FC	Amount in LC	Text
CoCode	0001	G/L acct	400020			Long text	Raw mat.consumed/trading goods without acct assgt					
03/30/2007	WL	49000124	03/30/2007	81		20070330			USD		824.45	
03/30/2007	WL	49000124	03/30/2007	81		20070330			USD		9,741.75	
03/30/2007	WL	49000124	03/30/2007	81		20070330			USD		0.81	
03/30/2007	WL	49000124	03/30/2007	81		20070330			USD		6,922.30	
03/30/2007	WL	49000124	03/30/2007	81		20070330			USD		2,306.70	
03/30/2007	WL	49000124	03/30/2007	81		20070330			USD		59.90	
03/30/2007	WL	49000124	03/30/2007	81		20070330			USD		14.90	
03/30/2007	WL	49000125	03/30/2007	81		20070330			USD		102,351.15	
03/30/2007	WL	49000125	03/30/2007	81		20070330			USD		10,782.00	
03/30/2007	WL	49000125	03/30/2007	81		20070330			USD		2,816.10	
03/30/2007	WL	49000125	03/30/2007	81		20070330			USD		7,506.00	
03/30/2007	WL	49000125	03/30/2007	81		20070330			USD		10,465.20	
03/30/2007	WL	49000125	03/30/2007	81		20070330			USD		8,788.00	
03/30/2007	WL	49000125	03/30/2007	81		20070330			USD		5,193.15	
03/30/2007	WL	49000125	03/30/2007	81		20070330			USD		4,148.85	
03/30/2007	WL	49000125	03/30/2007	81		20070330			USD		14,848.29	
03/30/2007	WL	49000125	03/30/2007	81		20070330			USD		10,132.00	
03/30/2007	WL	49000126	03/30/2007	81		20070330			USD		19,786.80	
03/30/2007	WL	49000126	03/30/2007	81		20070330			USD		3,896.70	
03/30/2007	WL	49000126	03/30/2007	81		20070330			USD		11,866.80	
03/30/2007	WL	49000126	03/30/2007	81		20070330			USD		1,537.80	
03/30/2007	WL	49000126	03/30/2007	81		20070330			USD		1,048.25	
03/30/2007	WL	49000126	03/30/2007	81		20070330			USD		81.95	
*									USD		235,119.85	
**									USD		235,119.85	
***									USD		235,119.85	

Figure 6.2 Standard SAP Report "Line Item Evaluation"

6.3.2 Accounts Payable Information System

You can use the accounts payable information system, among other things, to evaluate the payment history, the cash discount history, the exchange rate risk for vendors, or the vendor due date breakdown.

The following list describes typical reports in accounts payable accounting:

Typical reports in Accounts Payable Accounting

▶ **Due date analysis**

This report prepares the data for the due date breakdown. It considers items that are open on a key date. The amounts of these items are aggregated by the DUE and NOT DUE criteria. You can sort these values according to the DUE SINCE OR DUE IN criteria. When you create the evaluation, you can determine the intervals in days.

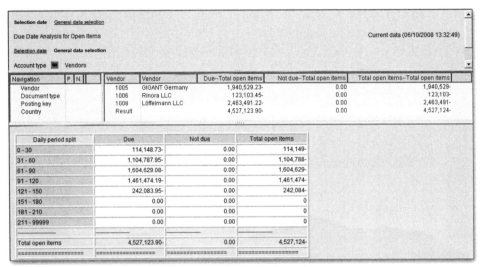

Figure 6.3 Standard SAP Report "Due Date Analysis"

▶ **Overdue items**
This report evaluates due items. It considers the items due on a key date. The overdue status is displayed based on days in arrears, amounts, and interest calculation numerators.

6.3.3 Reports in Materials Management

Purchase orders issued as well as any other purchasing documents must be carefully checked while they are processed.

Periodic purchase order monitoring
In periodic purchase order monitoring, the resubmission interval of all purchase requisitions, offers, scheduling agreement schedule lines, and purchase orders is checked, and dunning notices are automatically printed. In addition, you can perform targeted purchase order monitoring by evaluating the purchase order history via the quantity-based receipt, and quality checks during goods receipt inspection.

Additional evaluations
You can also create evaluation reports in the operational tactical purchasing management for the following:

- Items (e.g., ABC analysis)
- Vendors (e.g., purchase order value)
- Purchasing groups (e.g., purchase value)
- All purchasing documents (e.g., all purchase requisitions for a material)

6.3.4 Purchasing Information System

The purchasing information system is a tool you can use to collect, aggregate, and evaluate data from purchasing processing. In addition to flexible analyses based on the information structure in the Data Dictionary (see Figure 6.4), you can compare important key figures using standard analyses by comparing actual figures and planning figures.

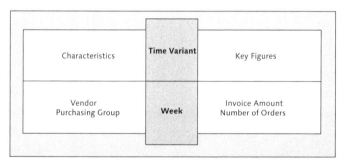

Figure 6.4 Information Structure of the Purchasing Information System

The following list describes some reports as examples:

- **Purchasing group**
  You can directly access this analysis via the purchasing group. For example, you might ask the following question: What is the purchase order value of a purchasing group with regard to a specific vendor?

Reports in the purchasing information system

Purch. group	PO value		Invoice Amount		Purchase orders
Total	14,638,271.90	USD	3,966,754.29	USD	178
Buyer TRADIGOOD	12,246,868.72	USD	3,966,754.29	USD	75
Buyer SEMFIGOOD	2,391,403.18	USD	0.00	USD	103

Figure 6.5 Standard SAP Report "Purchasing Group"

▸ **Vendor**

A vendor analysis makes sense if you want to directly access data relating to a vendor. For example, you might ask the following question: Which materials and which quantities were ordered from a vendor?

Vendor	PO value		Invoice Amount		Order quantity	
Total	14,638,271.90	USD	3,966,754.29	USD	785,251.000	***
HOELL Inc.	299,932.05	USD	0.00	USD	10,457	PC
Apple Bike Inc.	387,455.38	USD	0.00	USD	110,903	PC
GIANT Bicycles	8,812,630.42	USD	1,632,721.97	USD	17,938	PC
Rinora Llc.	100,344.83	USD	103,448.28	USD	1	PC
Sheet Copper Llc.	379,169.50	USD	0.00	USD	87,560	PC
John Nash Llc.	2,750,253.72	USD	2,230,584.04	USD	56,892	PC
Whell America Inc.	269,074.64	USD	0.00	USD	143,164.000	***
Steelworks Inc.	339,789.99	USD	0.00	USD	239,390	PC
Walliger & Sons	484,830.50	USD	0.00	USD	500	PC
Alufix Inc.	570,084.79	USD	0.00	USD	37,296	PC
Rubber Sales Llc.	244,705.48	USD	0.00	USD	81,150	PC

Figure 6.6 Standard SAP Report "Vendor"

▸ **Material group**

This analysis enables direct access via the material group. The analysis answers the following question, for example: What is the number of the purchase order items with regard to a material group?

Material group	PO value		Invoice amount		Order quantity	
Total	14,638,271.90	USD	3,966,754.29	USD	785,251.000	***
AG Brake	201,123.40	USD	0.00	USD	56,636	PC
AG Handle Bar	20,006.44	USD	0.00	USD	10,120	PC
AG Frame	860,515.32	USD	0.00	USD	33,366	PC
AG Wheel	595,853.69	USD	0.00	USD	340,540	PC
AG Hook-up	397,543.38	USD	0.00	USD	118,903	PC
AG Equipment	316,360.95	USD	0.00	USD	196,534.000	***
Component Part	2,269,310.15	USD	2,065,517.32	USD	22	PC
TG Children Bike	3,675,246.85	USD	0.00	USD	7,433	PC
TG Mountain Bike	484,830.50	USD	0.00	USD	500	PC
TG Trekking Bike	5,517,548.57	USD	1,901,236.97	USD	10,740	PC
TG Equipment	299,932.65	USD	0.00	USD	10,457	PC

Figure 6.7 Standard SAP Report "Material Group"

▸ **Material**

You should always use the material analysis if you want to access statistical data that is directly related to a material. A possible question for material analysis could be: Which material and quantities thereof was ordered?

Material	PO value		Order quantity		GR quantity	
Total	14,638,271.90	USD	785,251.000	***	671,073.000	***
Spoke RB	3,136.00	USD	160,000	PC	160,000	PC
Spoke MB	1,176.00	USD	60,000	PC	0	PC
Brake Handle RB	118,316.80	USD	31,136	PC	31,136	PC
Rubber Grup RB	19,198.72	USD	30,450	PC	30,450	PC
Circle RB	148,192.72	USD	27,040	PC	27,040	PC
Liner RB	185,949.00	USD	27,000	PC	27,000	PC
Gear Cable ahead	9,626.33	USD	21,115	PC	21,115	PC
Spoke Reflector	2,793.60	USD	18,000	PC	6,300	PC
Rubber Grup MB	9,907.96	USD	15,960	PC	12,180	PC
Hub rear RB	52,393.97	USD	15,840	PC	15,840	PC
Rest	14,087,580.80	USD	378,710.000	***	340,012.000	***

Figure 6.8 Standard SAP Report "Material"

6.3.5 Vendor Evaluation

You can implement a vendor evaluation based on the vendor evaluation system. Here, a scoring model is used to assess vendors according to standardized criteria.

If required, the four main criteria of price, quality, delivery, and service can be extended, individually weighted, and subdivided into multiple subcriteria. To determine the scores, the system consults already existing data and manually entered scores. This enables you to provide your own positive or negative experiences.

Criteria for vendor evaluation

Vendor	QtyRl.1	QtyRl.2	OTDel.1	OTDel.2	CShpIn1	CShpIn2
Total	100	100	82	72	0	0
HOELL Inc.	100	100	95	55	0	0
Apple Bike Inc.	100	100	90	77	0	0
GIANT Bicycles	100	100	43	39	0	0
Rinora Llc.	100	100	60	60	0	0
Sheet Copper Llc.	100	100	82	72	0	0
John Nash Llc.	100	100	77	71	0	0
Whell America Inc.	100	100	89	86	0	0
Steelworks Inc.	100	100	85	67	0	0
Walliger & Sons	100	100	95	93	0	0
Alufix Llc.	100	100	95	87	0	0
Rubber Sales Llc.	100	100	84	63	0	0

Figure 6.9 Standard SAP Report "Vendor Evaluation"

Using this analysis you can track, for example, whether a specific vendor delivers the material on time and in the desired quantity. The key figures available for evaluation are the scores for the criteria, including quantity reliability, on-time delivery performance, deviation from shipping notification (compliance with confirmation date), shipping instructions, and quality audit (is currently not updated).

Materials and services

You can use the vendor evaluation for procurement controlling of both materials and services:

▸ **Procurement of materials**
The selection of supply sources and the continuous check of existing vendor relationships can be supported. You are provided with information about the best prices, payment and delivery terms. You can determine possible problems that may occur during procurement and resolve them in cooperation with the respective vendor, based on detailed information.

▸ **Procurement of services**
For each plant, you can check the reliability of vendors from whom you procure services. You can also determine the quality of the service and whether a specific vendor performs the services on the requested date.

▸ **Scores and criteria**
A score system with points from 1 to 100 is available, which you can deploy to measure vendor performance with regard to five main evaluation criteria. Based on the overall score, you can get a general impression of the vendor's performance and compare it to others.

▸ **Evaluation reports**
For example, you can generate ranking lists of the best vendors according to the overall score and with regard to a specific material. Evaluation changes are recorded in logs.

6.3.6 Inventory Controlling

Inventory controlling is closely linked to inventory management because you must ensure a sufficient warehouse service level and a moderate degree of tied-up capital.

Key figures for inventory management

The functions of inventory controlling enable you to determine meaningful inventory management key figures (see Figure 6.10).

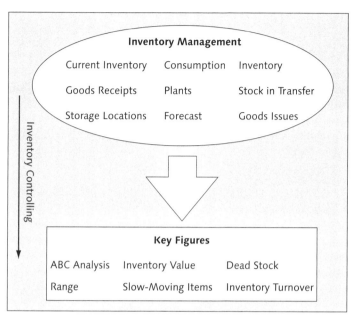

Figure 6.10 Inventory Controlling

The analysis area can be delimited by different analysis objects such as plant, period of time, material type, and so on. The results can be checked by providing lists or they can be illustrated in two or three-dimensional graphics. Cause studies can be implemented via *drilldown*. Here, you can resolve aggregated key figures all the way to individual material movements, including the display of the material documents.

Material	Val.stk rec qty		Val.stk iss qty		Total usage	
Total	692,835.000	***	2,649,640.200	***	2,649,641.200	***
Spoke RB	160,000	PC	1,002,672	PC	1,002,672	PC
Spoke MB	0	PC	509,940	PC	509,940	PC
Spoke Reflector	6,300	PC	84,034	PC	84,034	PC
Cable	5,000	M	44,506.200	M	44,506.200	M
Rubber Grup RD	30,450	PC	27,852	PC	27,852	PC
Brake Handle RB	31,136	PC	27,852	PC	27,852	PC
Pedal	8,000	PC	27,852	PC	27,852	PC
Circle RB	27,040	PC	27,852	PC	27,852	PC
Tube RB	4,180	PC	27,852	PC	27,852	PC
Liner RB	27,000	PC	27,852	PC	27,852	PC
Rest	393,729.000	***	841,376.000	***	841,377.000	***

Figure 6.11 Standard SAP Report "Material Analysis"

6.4   Individual Reporting

Procurement controlling's goal is to identify the utilization of the pro-
curement business process from MM or e-procurement as compared to
Financial Accounting (FI). Such evaluation is not possible in standard
SAP reports.

MM usage rate   Therefore, for controlling the utilization of the MM component and the
e-procurement system, you require an individual report that evaluates
the relevant information by processing procurement transactions in real
time. The goal is to document the *MM usage rate* in comparison to Financial Accounting (FI).

The MM usage rate can be determined by analyzing the posting transactions of those accounts in which procurements should only be made
from the MM component or the e-procurement system. The concepts
of such MM accounts, for example, the DP materials account, are predefined via an MM target ratio. For the specified account, the posting
must be carried out via the MM component; consequently, the MM target ratio is 100%.

The evaluation of the MM usage rate should contain the respective percentages of purchase orders that were posted via vendor invoices (Financial Accounting (FI) component), and via SAP SRM or MM. This can
be implemented with a different degree of detail via different reporting tools of the SAP system or SAP NetWeaver BI system, which are
described in the following sections.

The MM or SRM usage rate for processing procurement transactions
can be implemented by analyzing posting transactions on the MM or
SRM accounts. Such MM accounts should be documented in a target
concept with regard to their use (e.g., procurements only from the MM
component).

6.4.1   Usage Rate of MM and SRM

To determine the usage rate of MM or Financial Accounting (FI) (MM or
FI ratio), the following is assumed:

▶ The MM ratio is the percentage of procurement-relevant transactions that are processed via the MM component. It therefore indicates the percentage of goods and services in the overall procurement volume that were procured via MM or SRM. Ideally, the MM ratio is 100%.

▶ For determining the MM ratio, you only consider transactions that were posted on accounts which were identified as MM-mandatory in a target concept (MM target ratio).

▶ The MM target ratio is established individually for each MM account and reflects the expectations with regard to the utilization of the MM component for the respective account. The MM target ratio can be readily adapted to changed expectations.

▶ Additionally, the MM ratio is split into the MM ratio (ERP) and the MM ratio (SRM) to control the utilization of the SRM component for specific MM accounts.

▶ The FI ratio is the percentage of procurement-relevant transactions that are processed via the Financial Accounting (FI) component. Ideally, the FI ratio is almost 0%.

Another differentiation of the MM ratio could be as follows:

MM ratio 1 shows the percentage of the vendor invoices in MM for the overall volume of vendor invoices in MM and Financial Accounting (FI) in the respective company code.

MM ratio 2 reflects the percentage of the procurement transactions of consumption goods that was processed via the MM component on accounts, and for which – according to the target concept – the utilization of the MM component is mandatory. In the ideal case, the MM ratio is 100%.

6.4.2 Solution 1: SAP Query with Calculated Key Figures

The first solution is provided with *SAP Query*. It enables you to define individual reports and lists based on various SAP tables.

With two-dimensional reports, attributes are provided in columns and the characteristics of these attribute are shown in rows (see Figure 6.12). Additionally, you can integrate customer-specific tables, which would

Two-dimensional reports

be necessary for the MM target ratio, for example. This key figure had to be recorded and stored in a separate SAP table for each MM account and each SRM account. Moreover, you could define calculated key figures (for example, MM usage rate) and calculate and include those in the report in addition to the key figures that already exist in the SAP system (for example, value of the resource items).

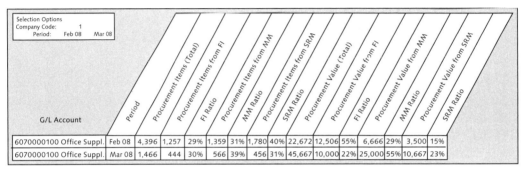

Figure 6.12 Design of an SAP Query

MM and SRM ratio   To control the MM or SRM ratio, you can consult an SAP query that is restricted to the following basic information:

▶ Period

▶ Total procurement items

▶ Procurement items from Financial Accounting (FI)

▶ FI ratio

▶ Procurement items from MM

▶ MM ratio

▶ Procurement items from SRM

▶ SRM ratio

▶ Total procurement value

▶ Procurement value from Financial Accounting (FI)

▶ FI ratio

▶ Procurement value from MM

▶ MM ratio

▸ Procurement value from SRM

▸ SRM ratio

The SAP query could have the following structure:

To restrict the SAP query, in the initial screen you could enter the selection criteria PERIOD (MONTH/YEAR), COMPANY CODE, and G/L ACCOUNT as required. The system always displays results relating to the value of the selected dimensions (period, company code, etc.). If no restrictions exist, the results are provided for the entire live system.

Selecting the restrictions

On the basis of the displayed results in the report, drilldown to the line item reports is possible. These reports contain account assignments, such as cost center, internal orders, commitment item, and so on, which are not included in the MM usage rate report. The account assignments are not included in this SAP query intentionally, because with this display of the SAP query an increasing number of attributes results in a less clear report. The required values can then be taken from the line item for investigation.

It is not recommended to display the target MM and SRM ratios because you must create a customer-specific table to determine these values. This would unnecessarily increase the development effort. The target values must be maintained regularly and can differ for each organizational unit. In addition, the target entries are unique. For MM and SRM accounts, the target MM and SRM ratios should be 100%.

Target MM and SRM ratios

SAP query is characterized by good performance, because it uses pre-aggregated SAP tables.

6.4.3 Solution 2: Analysis in the Logistics Information System (LIS)

By default, the *Logistics Information System* (LIS) is a combination of different information systems in logistics, for example, the sales and purchasing information systems. Accounting information systems are not integrated by default, which means that you can't access information, communication and evaluation structures for accounting in the standard version; however, you can individually complement or define necessary structures.

Benefits of LIS   You can fulfill the following general requirements for a reporting tool by using the LIS:

▸ Direct availability in the SAP system

▸ Based on total values

▸ Period comparison options

▸ Flexibility in the column selection

▸ Drilldown functionality (for example, company code, G/L account, and CO account assignment)

▸ Available Excel interface

▸ Existing analysis functions (for example, top 10, filter values, exceptions, ABC analysis, and comparison of key figures)

You must consider the specific requirements of the report "MM usage rate" differently. To be evaluated, the information structures required here must contain corresponding attributes in the form of characteristics and key figures.

Characteristics   The following characteristics are available in the LIS for MM and SRM
in LIS   values:

▸ Period (month/year)

▸ Company code

▸ G/L account

▸ Cost center

▸ Internal order

▸ Commitment item

▸ Earmarked funds

▸ Material group (empty for Financial Accounting (FI) postings)

Key figures in LIS   The following key figures are available in the LIS for MM and SRM values:

▸ **Financial Accounting (FI) values**
Key figures are not included in the LIS and must be extracted individually from operational tables via reports, table access, or ABAP program.

▶ **MM values**

Key figures are included in the LIS by default.

▶ **SRM values**

Key figures are included in the LIS by default.

Additionally, the *MM target ratio* is output in percentages and currently not maintained in the SAP system for each G/L account. This information must be stored in a separate SAP table (Z table) and provided to the LIS for evaluation.

The report "MM usage rate" can be defined using a flexible analysis in the LIS, in which the characteristics and key figures are compiled and aggregated according to criteria to be determined. For report definition in the LIS, the SAP tools Report Writer or Report Painter are used.

MM usage rate

The data must be loaded at the end of the previous day to ensure a correct and complete display of the values in reports of the logistics information system. Consequently, the output values have the status of the previous day.

MM Usage Rate Report with Selection to the Day

The report lists key figures (number of line items, purchase order values, invoice values, and ratios) with regard to the utilization of MM as compared to Financial Accounting (FI). Here, the key figures are differentiated and displayed cumulatively according to characteristics (G/L accounts, company codes, cost centers, internal orders, commitment items, assets, and material groups).

The person responsible for the company code is provided with information to which extent MM accounts, which, according to the MM target concept, are mandatory, are posted from MM, the e-procurement system, and Financial Accounting (FI). Moreover, a complete view of MM utilization is possible with regard to different characteristics (for example, company codes or cost centers).

The report columns contain key figures relating to the MM usage rate from MM, the e-procurement system, and Financial Accounting (FI). The individual columns are described in Table 6.1.

Report columns

Figure 6.13 "MM Usage Rate" Report Columns (MM and SRM)

MM Usage Rate	ORDITEM MM	ORDNETVAL MM	ORDINVVAL MM	ORDITEM EBP	ORDNETVAL EBP	ORDINVVAL EBP
700000000 Power Supply Assets	0	0	0	0	0	0
770000000 Other Assets	0	0	0	0	0	0
840000000 Car Pool	5	101,000.00	117,000.00	6	10,200.00	0.00
850000000 Other Factory Equipment	0	0	0	0	0	0
860000000 Office Machines	0	0	0	8	2,862.23	746.46
870000000 Furniture	2	600.00	0.00	6	2,800.00	0.00
890000000 Low-value Factory	0	0	0	0	0	0
2080000000 Other Stocks	12	1,300.00	0.00	0	0	0
2120000000 Inventory	2	400.00	0.00	0	0	0
2130000000 Trading Goods	25	156,733.84	0.00	0	0	0
6000000000 Raw Materials	0	0	0	0	0	0
6020000000 Supplies	2	2.00	0.00	0	0	0
6030000000 Operating Materials	0	0	0	0	0	0
6030000101 Winter Grittings	0	0	0	0	0	0
6070000000 Other Purchases	70	42,183.02	41,188.80	4	70.00	0.00
6070000100 Office Equipment	0	0	0	34	8,477.62	9,567.49
6070000200 DP / TC Materials	0	0	0	43	5,338.92	0.00
6120000300 Engineering Services	0	0	0	0	0	0
6130000000 External Services	1	1,160.00	0.00	0	0	0
6162000301 Software Maintenance	0	0	0	0	0	0
6162000900 Other Maintenance and	0	0	0	0	0	0
6170000220 Transportation	0	0	0	0	0	0
* G/L Accounts	119	303,386.86	158,188.80	101	29,748.77	10,313.95
* Company Codes	119	303,386.86	158,188.80	101	29,748.77	10,313.95
* Cost Centers	57	1,856.22	0.00	81	13,886.54	9,567.49
* Internal Orders	105	199,930.64	41,188.80	0	0	0
* Commitment Items	0	0	0	0	0	0
* Assets	7	101,600.00	117,000.00	20	15,062.23	746.46
* Material Groups	118	302,226.86	158,188.80	99	29,704.77	10,313.95

Figure 6.13 "MM Usage Rate" Report Columns (MM and SRM)

MM Usage Rate	INVITEM FI	INVVAL FI	MM Target Rat	MM Ratio Tot	MM Ratio (ERP)	MM Ratio (EBP)
700000000 Power Supply Assets	1	83.00	0.00	0.00	0.00	0.00
770000000 Other Assets	1	73.00	0.00	0.00	0.00	0.00
840000000 Car Pool	43	1,079,367.00	80.00	20.37	9.26	11.11
850000000 Other Factory Equipment	1	4.00	0.00	0.00	0.00	0.00
860000000 Office Machines	11	12,354.00	40.00	42.11	0.00	42.11
870000000 Furniture	0	0	50.00	100.00	25.00	75.00
890000000 Low-value Factory	1	300.00	0.00	0.00	0.00	0.00
2080000000 Other Stocks	0	0	100.00	100.00	100.00	0.00
2120000000 Inventory	0	0	0.00	100.00	100.00	0.00
2130000000 Trading Goods	0	0	100.00	100.00	100.00	0.00
6000000000 Raw Material	4	1,000.00	0.00	0.00	0.00	0.00
6020000000 Supplies	0	0	100.00	100.00	100.00	0.00
6030000000 Operating Materials	1	400.00	0.00	0.00	0.00	0.00
6030000101 Winter Grittings	1	100.00	0.00	0.00	0.00	0.00
6070000000 Other Purchases	1	1,000.00	80.00	98.67	93.33	5.33
6070000100 Office Equipment	60	89,332.94	100.00	36.17	0.00	36.17
6070000200 DP / TC Materials	1	450.00	100.00	97.73	0.00	97.73
6120000300 Engineering Services	1	99.00	0.00	0.00	0.00	0.00
6130000000 External Services	4	0	75.00	20.00	20.00	0.00
6162000301 Software Maintenance	0	0	80.00	0.00	0.00	0.00
6162000900 Other Maintenance and	4	4,224.30	0.00	0.00	0.00	0.00
6170000220 Transportation	0	0	30.00	0.00	0.00	0.00
* G/L Accounts	135		82.90	61.97	33.52	28.45
* Company Codes	135		82.90	61.97	33.52	28.45
* Cost Centers	69		84.71	66.67	27.54	39.13
* Internal Orders	7	14,509.91	86.38	93.75	93.75	0.00
* Commitment Items	2		0.00	0.00	0.00	0.00
* Assets	37	1,078,829.00	58.67	42.19	10.94	31.25
* Material Groups	0	0	85.11	100.00	54.38	45.62

Figure 6.14 "MM Usage Rate" Report Columns (FI and Ratios)

Column	Description
ORDITEM MM Purchase order items MM	The number of purchase order items contained in the purchase orders of MM is displayed cumulatively.
ORDNETVAL MM Net purchase order value MM	The cumulated value of purchase orders from MM (considering price reductions and surcharges) is displayed, with the net purchase order value determined by multiplying the order quantity by the purchase order price.
ORDINVVAL MM Invoice amount MM	The cumulated invoice amount of the purchase orders from MM is displayed. This is the sum of the previously recorded item amounts of an invoice or credit memo for a purchase order item, minus cash discounts, plus non-deductible input tax and unplanned delivery costs.
ORDITEM EBP Purchase order items e-procurement	The number of purchase order items contained in the purchase orders of e-procurement (SRM) is displayed cumulatively.
ORDNETVAL EBP Net purchase order value e-procurement	The cumulated value of the purchase orders from e-procurement (considering price reductions and surcharges) is displayed. The net purchase order value is determined by multiplying the order quantity by the purchase order price.
ORDINVVAL EBP Invoice amount e-procurement	The cumulated invoice amount of the purchase orders from e-procurement is displayed. This is the sum of the previously recorded item amounts of an invoice or credit memo for a purchase order item, minus cash discounts, plus non-deductible input tax and unplanned delivery costs.
INVITEM FI Invoice items Financial Accounting (FI)	The number of invoice items contained in the invoices of Financial Accounting (FI) is displayed cumulatively.

Table 6.1 Column Content of the "MM Usage Rate" Report

Column	Description
INVVAL FI Invoice amount Financial Accounting (FI)	The cumulated invoice amount of invoices from Financial Accounting (FI) is displayed, which is the total of the recorded line items of an invoice.
MM Target Rat.	The MM target ratio is established for each MM account and reflects the expectations with regard to the utilization of the MM component in the respective account. The MM target ratio can readily be adapted to changed expectations.
MM Ratio Tot.	The MM ratio is the percentage of procurement-relevant transactions that are processed via the MM component and e-procurement system. Ideally, the MM ratio is 100%.
MM Ratio (ERP)	The MM ratio (ERP) is the percentage of procurement-relevant transactions that were processed via the MM component.
MM Ratio (EBP)	The MM ratio (EBP) is the percentage of procurement-relevant transactions that were processed via the e-procurement system.
FI Ratio	The FI ratio is the percentage of procurement-relevant transactions that were processed via the Financial Accounting (FI) component.

Table 6.1 Column Content of the "MM Usage Rate" Report (Cont.)

In the rows of the report, the key figures from the columns can be displayed according to different characteristics.

"MM, SRM, and FI Ratios" Report with Annual Selection

This report lists the MM, SRM, and FI ratios in a separate report respectively, by a specific fiscal year. Here, the ratios are indicated in periods (per month) for each G/L account and company code.

MM ratio The MM ratio is the percentage of procurement-relevant transactions that were processed via the MM component (see Figure 6.15).

MM Ratio (ERP)		MM Ratio (Jan)	MM Ratio (Feb)	MM Ratio (Mar)	MM Ratio (Apr)	MM Ratio (May)	MM Ratio (Jun)
LIS-03: MM Ratio 2007 (periodically)			09/06/2007				Page: 2 / 2
Comany Codes from:	0001 to ZZZZ						
Documents Date from:	01/01/2007 to 12/31/2007						
700000000	Power Supply Assets	0.00	0.00	0.00	0.00	0.00	0.00
770000000	Other Assets	0.00	0.00	0.00	0.00	0.00	0.00
840000000	Car Pool	0.00	0.00	0.00	0.00	0.00	0.00
850000000	Other Factory Equipment	0.00	0.00	0.00	0.00	0.00	0.00
860000000	Office Machines	0.00	0.00	0.00	0.00	0.00	0.00
870000000	Furniture	0.00	0.00	0.00	100.00	0.00	0.00
890000000	Low-value Factory	0.00	0.00	0.00	0.00	0.00	0.00
2080000000	Other Stocks	100.00	100.00	0.00	0.00	0.00	0.00
2120000000	Inventory	0.00	0.00	100.00	0.00	0.00	0.00
2130000000	Trading Goods	0.00	0.00	100.00	0.00	0.00	100.00
6000000000	Raw Material	0.00	0.00	0.00	0.00	0.00	0.00
6020000000	Supplies	0.00	0.00	0.00	0.00	0.00	0.00
6030000000	Operating Materials	0.00	0.00	0.00	0.00	0.00	0.00
6030000101	Winter Grittings	0.00	0.00	0.00	0.00	0.00	0.00
6070000000	Other Purchases	0.00	100.00	100.00	100.00	0.00	0.00
6070000100	Office Equipment	0.00	0.00	0.00	0.00	0.00	0.00
6070000200	DP / TC Materials	0.00	0.00	0.00	0.00	0.00	0.00
6120000300	Engineering Services	0.00	0.00	0.00	0.00	0.00	0.00
6130000900	External Services	0.00	0.00	0.00	0.00	100.00	0.00
6162000900	Other Maintenance and	0.00	0.00	0.00	0.00	0.00	0.00
* G/L Accounts		11.94	67.37	57.63	50.00	12.50	25.00
2280 Company Code		0.00	0.00	0.00	0.00	0.00	0.00
2290 Company Code		0.00	0.00	0.00	0.00	0.00	0.00
2300 Company Code		0.00	0.00	0.00	0.00	0.00	0.00
2314 Company Code		0.00	0.00	0.00	0.00	0.00	0.00
2400 Company Code		0.00	0.00	0.00	0.00	0.00	0.00
2410 Company Code		0.00	0.00	0.00	0.00	0.00	0.00
2420 Company Code		0.00	0.00	0.00	0.00	0.00	0.00
2515 Company Code		100.00	94.12	97.30	100.00	100.00	100.00
2610 Company Code		0.00	0.00	0.00	0.00	0.00	0.00
2640 Company Code		0.00	0.00	0.00	0.00	0.00	0.00
2806 Company Code		0.00	0.00	0.00	0.00	0.00	0.00
2850 Company Code		0.00	0.00	0.00	0.00	0.00	0.00
2900 Company Code		0.00	0.00	0.00	0.00	0.00	0.00
2920 Company Code		0.00	0.00	0.00	0.00	0.00	0.00
* Company Codes		11.94	67.37	59.02	50.00	22.22	25.00

Figure 6.15 "MM Ratios" Report Columns (Periodic Consideration)

The SRM ratio is the percentage of procurement-relevant transactions that were processed via the e-procurement system (see Figure 6.16).

SRM ratio

EBP Ratio		EBP Ratio(Jan)	EBP Ratio(Feb)	EBP Ratio(Mar)	EBP Ratio(Apr)	EBP Ratio(May)	EBP Ratio(Jun)
700000000	Power Supply Assets	0.00	0.00	0.00	0.00	0.00	0.00
770000000	Other Assets	0.00	0.00	0.00	0.00	0.00	0.00
840000000	Car Pool	42.86	0.00	0.00	0.00	0.00	0.00
850000000	Other Factory Equipment	0.00	0.00	0.00	0.00	0.00	0.00
860000000	Office Machines	33.33	100.00	0.00	0.00	0.00	0.00
870000000	Furniture	100.00	100.00	0.00	0.00	0.00	0.00
890000000	Low-value Factory	0.00	0.00	0.00	0.00	0.00	0.00
2080000000	Other Stocks	0.00	0.00	0.00	0.00	0.00	0.00
2120000000	Inventory	0.00	0.00	0.00	0.00	0.00	0.00
2130000000	Trading Goods	0.00	0.00	0.00	0.00	0.00	0.00
6000000000	Raw Material	0.00	0.00	0.00	0.00	0.00	0.00
6020000000	Supplies	0.00	0.00	0.00	0.00	0.00	0.00
6030000000	Operating Materials	0.00	0.00	0.00	0.00	0.00	0.00
6030000101	Winter Grittings	0.00	0.00	0.00	0.00	0.00	0.00
6070000000	Other Purchases	100.00	0.00	0.00	0.00	0.00	0.00
6070000100	Office Equipment	0.00	81.82	100.00	66.67	100.00	0.00
6070000200	DP / TC Materials	100.00	100.00	94.12	0.00	0.00	100.00
6120000300	Engineering Services	0.00	0.00	0.00	0.00	0.00	0.00
6130000900	External Services	0.00	0.00	0.00	0.00	0.00	0.00
6162000900	Other Maintenance and	0.00	0.00	0.00	0.00	0.00	0.00
* G/L Accounts		59.70	27.37	37.29	25.00	75.00	25.00
2280 Company Code		0.00	0.00	0.00	0.00	0.00	0.00
2290 Company Code		0.00	0.00	0.00	0.00	0.00	0.00
2300 Company Code		0.00	0.00	0.00	0.00	0.00	0.00
2314 Company Code		0.00	0.00	0.00	0.00	0.00	0.00
2400 Company Code		0.00	0.00	0.00	0.00	0.00	0.00
2410 Company Code		0.00	100.00	0.00	0.00	0.00	0.00
2420 Company Code		100.00	100.00	100.00	100.00	100.00	100.00
2515 Company Code		0.00	0.00	0.00	0.00	0.00	0.00
2610 Company Code		0.00	100.00	0.00	0.00	0.00	0.00
2640 Company Code		0.00	0.00	0.00	0.00	0.00	0.00
2806 Company Code		0.00	0.00	0.00	0.00	0.00	0.00
2850 Company Code		0.00	0.00	0.00	0.00	0.00	0.00
2900 Company Code		0.00	0.00	0.00	0.00	0.00	0.00
2920 Company Code		0.00	0.00	0.00	0.00	0.00	0.00
* Company Codes		59.70	27.37	36.07	25.00	66.67	25.00

Figure 6.16 "EBP Ratios" Report Columns (Periodic Consideration)

FI ratio   The FI ratio is the percentage of procurement-relevant transactions that were processed via the Financial Accounting (FI) component (see Figure 6.17).

FI Ratio	FI Ratio (Jan)	FI Ratio (Feb)	FI Ratio (Mar)	FI Ratio (Apr)	FI Ratio (May)	FI Ratio (Jun)
700000000 Power Supply Assets	100.00	0.00	0.00	0.00	0.00	0.00
770000000 Other Assets	100.00	0.00	0.00	0.00	0.00	0.00
840000000 Car Pool	57.14	100.00	100.00	100.00	100.00	100.00
850000000 Other Factory Equipment	100.00	0.00	0.00	0.00	0.00	0.00
860000000 Office Machines	66.67	0.00	0.00	0.00	0.00	0.00
870000000 Furniture	0.00	0.00	0.00	0.00	0.00	0.00
800000000 Low-value Factory	0.00	0.00	0.00	0.00	0.00	0.00
2090000000 Other Stocks	0.00	0.00	0.00	0.00	0.00	0.00
2120000000 Inventory	0.00	0.00	0.00	0.00	0.00	0.00
2130000000 Trading Goods	0.00	0.00	0.00	0.00	0.00	0.00
6000000000 Raw Material	0.00	0.00	0.00	0.00	0.00	0.00
6020000000 Supplies	0.00	0.00	0.00	0.00	0.00	0.00
6030000000 Operating Materials	0.00	0.00	0.00	0.00	0.00	0.00
6030000101 Winter Brittings	0.00	0.00	100.00	0.00	0.00	0.00
6070000000 Other Purchases	0.00	0.00	0.00	0.00	0.00	0.00
6070000100 Office Equipment	0.00	18.18	0.00	33.33	0.00	0.00
6070000200 DP / TC Materials	0.00	0.00	5.88	0.00	0.00	0.00
6120000300 Engineering Services	0.00	0.00	0.00	0.00	0.00	100.00
6130000900 External Services	0.00	0.00	0.00	0.00	0.00	0.00
6162000900 Other Maintenance and	0.00	0.00	0.00	0.00	0.00	0.00
* G/L Accounts	28.36	5.26	5.08	25.00	12.50	50.00
2280 Company Code	0.00	0.00	0.00	0.00	0.00	0.00
2290 Company Code	100.00	0.00	0.00	0.00	0.00	0.00
2300 Company Code	0.00	0.00	0.00	0.00	0.00	0.00
2314 Company Code	0.00	0.00	0.00	0.00	0.00	0.00
2400 Company Code	100.00	100.00	100.00	100.00	100.00	100.00
2410 Company Code	0.00	0.00	0.00	0.00	0.00	0.00
2420 Company Code	0.00	0.00	0.00	0.00	0.00	0.00
2515 Company Code	0.00	5.88	2.70	0.00	0.00	0.00
2610 Company Code	100.00	0.00	100.00	0.00	0.00	100.00
2640 Company Code	0.00	0.00	0.00	0.00	0.00	0.00
2806 Company Code	0.00	0.00	0.00	0.00	0.00	0.00
2850 Company Code	0.00	0.00	0.00	0.00	0.00	0.00
2900 Company Code	0.00	0.00	0.00	100.00	0.00	0.00
2920 Company Code	0.00	0.00	0.00	0.00	0.00	0.00
* Company Codes	28.36	5.26	4.92	25.00	11.11	50.00

Figure 6.17 "FI Ratio" Report Columns (Periodic Consideration)

The columns of the report display the MM, SRM, or FI ratios for a certain period (month). The respective key figure is indicated cumulatively for each month.

In the report rows, the key figures from the columns can be displayed according to G/L accounts and company codes.

6.5   SAP NetWeaver Business Intelligence

SAP NetWeaver Business Intelligence (SAP NetWeaver BI) is the data warehouse solution of SAP. It has been developed explicitly for data storage and data analysis. The integration of SAP data and external data is a fundamental component of this solution. Therefore, the target audience of SAP NetWeaver BI can include all employees of an enterprise.

In contrast to the other SAP report tools, this solution entails a real data warehouse approach, that is, data is provided in a system designed specifically for data analysis. The metadata schema has a cross-application concept and data is supplied consistently. Unlike other providers, SAP offers its data warehouse as a complete solution. This means that not just a few business areas are provided with templates for data analysis, but all information required in the enterprise is stored in predefined business-relevant data models.

Data warehouse approach

For this purpose, SAP NetWeaver BI includes Business Content (BC), which is quite comprehensive with predefined extraction and analysis models. It contains reports and roles, as well as required extractors for SAP data, data storage, and transformation and load processes to provide data for the information models.

Business Content

SAP NetWeaver BI also offers a business-relevant solution library called the Data Warehouse Library (DWL). The concept of the library is based primarily on BC. Together with the metadata model, it constitutes the actual content of the DWL. Users are provided with structures, which can be selected and adapted flexibly. These can then be used as the basis for loading data into the data warehouse. The library is complemented by analysis methods, technologies, and procedures, such as exception reporting and drill-through. From this range of functions, the user must select the required components.

Data Warehouse Library

SAP enables an easy connection to SAP ERP systems and an integrated metadata database system via BC included in SAP NetWeaver BI. Through the selection of information models from BC it is possible to quickly obtain first results. The use of predefined templates is viable because up to 80% of time and effort for a DW project is taken up by the selection and transformation of data. The goal is to map 80% of the functions with 20% of the effort, using the templates. This enables enterprises that are still at the developing stage of DW to quickly obtain an initial solution, provided that the predefined solution includes the required functions and offers the flexibility required for extensions.

Connection to SAP ERP

After implementation, the initial solution is continuously adapted to the changes at the organizational and IT levels. In a DWL, the restructuring of functions and business processes must be implemented promptly.

Adaptations

<table>
<tr><td>

Change Management

Changes to Customizing or master data within the SAP system directly affects SAP NetWeaver BI and defined reports.

Here, a distinction is made between two different types of changes:

▸ Changes that are automatically updated during the data loading process in SAP NetWeaver BI (e.g., additional cost centers and purchase orders)

▸ Changes that require manual adaptation of the reports in SAP NetWeaver BI (e.g., changed/additional master data structures and Customizing)

In the first case, data is updated in SAP NetWeaver BI through monthly data loading processes. If, for example, the cost object structure of a cost center changes, the cost center is responsible for an additional internal order as of the next period, the transaction data posted to this internal order is automatically considered in the relevant reports. This also applies to additional cost centers that are provided in the reports for evaluation after successful data loading.

In the second case, changes in SAP NetWeaver BI are mandatory to ensure data consistency.

For the mentioned data changes, you must initiate a communication process between the initiating and changing location in the SAP system and the team responsible for SAP NetWeaver BI.

</td></tr>
</table>

6.5.1 Standard Queries in SAP NetWeaver BI

BC in NetWeaver BI includes preconfigured objects. Hence, information models for different application areas are provided that contain technical preconfigurations and predefined workbooks, queries (reports), key figures, and characteristics.

Based on application-specific BC of procurement (supply chain management area) as well as e-procurement (supplier relationship management area), the following lists describe several standard queries that can be used for procurement controlling:

Procurement

▸ **Purchase order items**
This query lets you display both the purchase order value and the number of purchase order items whose desired delivery date has been confirmed. As a result, you can, for example, analyze to which extent a vendor has committed himself to the date preferred.

▶ **Purchase order quantities**

This query lets you identify and track discrepancies between ordered values and the values invoiced or received.

▶ **Ordering activities**

With this query, you can display purchasing activities for materials and vendors. This enables you to answer the following questions, for example: How often is a material ordered? How often is a material procured from a vendor? How is a material usually ordered – via purchase order, scheduling agreement, or contract?

▶ **Purchase order values**

With this query, you can evaluate the purchasing activities for a material considering the following questions, for example: How much money was spent for the procurement of a material in a plant or in total? How much was ordered from a vendor?

▶ **Vendor evaluation**

This query enables you to display the overall vendor score from the purchasing vendor evaluation, as well as its development. You can compare vendors considering different questions: Which vendor has the best overall score? To what extent has the overall score of a vendor changed in the past?

E-Procurement

▶ **Purchase orders**

Evaluation reports for purchase orders indicate which purchase orders have been posted within a specific period of time for each cost center and G/L account. Moreover, information about items and account assignment is documented.

▶ **Invoices**

This query indicates for each cost center and G/L account which invoices have been posted with balanced gross amounts (invoice minus credit memo) and quantities within a specific period.

▶ **Cost center account assignment**

With this query, the person responsible for a cost center is provided with an analysis to evaluate the value-based debit of the cost center for the current calendar month. Moreover, you can also analyze additional information, such as the requester or the types of applications (via the debited G/L account).

You can use the standard queries from preconfigured BC as templates for individual queries. You can also define cross-application queries including data from procurement, e-procurement, and Financial Accounting (FI).

6.5.2 MM Usage Report in SAP NetWeaver BI

The solution in the SAP system using SAP query has some restrictions with regard to requirements. These restrictions include, for example, drilldown to different levels of detail (company code, period, etc.) or waiving of selected account assignments (cost center, internal order, etc.).

To cover all report requirements, you can also use SAP NetWeaver BI as an implementation tool. The development of such a report in the SAP ERP system entails an unreasonably high effort.

Flexibility in the presentation
Thanks to the presentation flexibility in SAP NetWeaver BI, you can define optically appealing, multi-dimensional reports that allow for period and organization comparisons (see Figure 6.18).

MM Usage Report			Actual Ratio	Target Ratio	CoCd 0001	CoCd 0002	CoCd 0003
		Absolute					
All Accounts	Procurement Item	13,188	100%	100%	6,735	4,743	1,710
	FI	3,771	29%	0%	1,368	702	1,701
	MM	4,077	31%	0%	2,367	1,701	9
	SRM	5,340	40%	0%	3,000	2,340	0
	Procurement Value	68,016	100%	100%	27,000	19,320	21,696
	FI	37,518	55%	0%	USD 13,500	USD 10,320	USD 13,698
	MM	19,998	29%	0%	USD 9,000	USD 3,000	USD 7,998
	SRM	10,500	15%	0%	USD 4,500	USD 6,000	USD 0
6070000100 Office Supplies	Procurement Item	4,396	100%	100%	2,245	1,581	570
	FI	1,257	29%	0%	456	234	567
	MM	1,359	31%	0%	789	567	3
	SRM	1,780	40%	0%	1,000	780	0
	Procurement Value	USD 22,672	100%	100%	USD 9,000	USD 6,440	USD 7,232
	FI	USD 12,506	55%	0%	USD 4,500	USD 3,440	USD 4,566
	MM	USD 6,666	29%	0%	USD 3,000	USD 1,000	USD 2,666
	SRM	USD 3,500	15%	0%	USD 1,500	USD 2,000	USD 0

Figure 6.18 Draft of an SAP Query for MM Usage

In terms of possible further report requirements and the required definition of individual reports in the SAP ERP system, you should consider using SAP NetWeaver BI for the medium term in every project.

6.5.3   Management Reports in SAP NetWeaver BI

The introduction of SAP NetWeaver BI means that a data warehouse system is implemented in addition to the existing SAP ERP system to support management in the decision-making and strategic orientation of the enterprise through a subject-oriented, integrated, time-based, and permanent dataset.

The reason for extending and supplementing an SAP ERP reporting system is that the options to transfer data of an SAP ERP system to holistic and integrated reports are limited. For lack of sufficient interfaces, this could only be implemented through extension programming and manual interventions. However, this procedure could potentially not meet the requirements expected of the enterprise-wide base of data. Response times for complex queries would be too long and would put a heavy load on the operational SAP ERP system.

Restrictions of the SAP ERP system

This results from the numerous linking operations in a relational database for multidimensional queries. Additionally, serious problems arise for pending release changes, because the modified data structures must be transferred to the new release in case of data migration. To enable this, you must also maintain the extension programming in the new program to be able to call cross-department reports. The effort required would completely exceed the benefits.

Replacing the SAP ERP reporting is also supported by well-known ERP providers who shift their standard reporting systems successively to the data warehouse area. The reason for this is that reports in a data warehouse can be defined and maintained more easily.

In the basic structure of the information system for the support of decision makers, procurement controlling maintains the controlling-relevant dataset and evaluates the data in line with the information requirements of controlling.

7 Summary and Outlook

The chapters of this book clearly showed that implementing the procurement functions of the SAP solutions in a non-selective way is unproductive and doesn't allow for optimal solutions with regard to efficiency and the documentation of process management. When optimizing processes, organizational structures, and roles in procurement, you should therefore consider the entire scope of functions of the SAP solutions. If you concentrate only on the SAP ERP system's comprehensive scope of functions, this could result in inefficient procurement processing for some goods. Consequently, optimization requires using the e-procurement options and, depending on the type of goods to be procured, has to be coordinated with the various systems.

Selecting a procurement solution

Enterprises that are about to implement an SAP ERP system should seize the opportunity and consider using the SAP ERP and SAP SRM functions in parallel. The often-used strategy to first implement SAP ERP and then SAP SRM results in an imbalance that is problematic for several reasons.

Utilization of SAP ERP and SAP SRM

For the procurement of basic standard requirements (MRO items, indirect goods, etc.), the SAP ERP system's MM component offers fully functional coverage. However, conventional procurement with full logistical documentation results in high administrative costs. The second procurement option – using the Financial Accounting (FI) component – offers "lean" system-supported procurement processing, but doesn't provide sufficient documentation (see Figure 7.1). To ensure adherence to compliance guidelines and to create revision-proof process documentation, you can only use the procurement functions in the SAP ERP system's MM component.

The use of the MM component presupposes the creation of suitable master data structures, authorizations in the SAP ERP system, and the creation of an appropriate procurement organization with operational purchasers at suitable locations within the enterprise. Due to the necessary initial effort, the suboptimal overall nature of the solution, and its temporary character, this procedure is problematic. This is underscored by master data that is created in the SAP ERP system and that becomes obsolete in the expected implementation of the SAP SRM system and therefore needs to be removed. A master dataset that does not meet the operational requirements reduces the operability of the system (for example, due to longer search times). Moreover, this causes unnecessary – and, due to in-depth integration at times considerable – process costs (for example, by triggering purchase orders with incorrect master data).

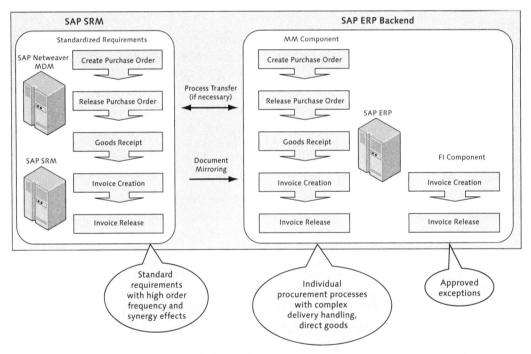

Figure 7.1 Distribution of the Procurement Processes across SAP ERP and SAP SRM

Implementation of SAP SRM The procedure for the implementation of SAP SRM does not change, irrespective of whether enterprises already use SAP ERP or perform a new implementation. As with any other software implementation, profitability considerations are important. E-procurement is characterized by high investment costs and considerable operating costs, but it can also lead to a clear reduction in process costs and, to a certain degree, procurement costs.

The profitability analysis should determine whether the potential for reducing process and procurement costs justifies the high investment and high operating costs. Therefore, you must carry out requirements and vendor analyses. The goal of the first analysis is to determine whether the requirement range includes catalog-capable goods with sufficient order frequency. Instead of the procurement volume, the number of different procurement transactions is the decision factor here. There is a significant difference between procuring 3,000 folders for one consumer once and implementing 300 procurement processes with ten folders each over a specific period and across the entire enterprise.

Profitability analysis

The goal of the vendor analysis is to analyze the ability of individual vendors to enable Internet-based procurement of goods that are categorized as catalog-capable. Vendors' inability to provide products in an electronic catalog that is based on accepted standards makes the use of any e-procurement system impossible. Particularly for special requirements, such as lubricants or illuminants, there can still be bottlenecks on the vendor market, ten years after the use of the first e-procurement solutions.

Vendor analysis

In light of increased compliance requirements and possible data fragmentation when different procurement variants are used, the development of a powerful reporting system based on *SAP NetWeaver Business Intelligence* (SAP NetWeaver BI) has gained in significance.

The SAP NetWeaver BI system is characterized by many different functions that are not available in the standard reporting of the SAP ERP system. For example, reports can be created web-enabled and distributed via a portal. You can also install an alert system with which you can automatically send emails to the procurement controller if predefined threshold values are exceeded (e.g. *MM ratios*, see Section 6.4.1, Usage Rate of MM and SRM).

SAP NetWeaver BI

Not least due to relocation and further development of component-related as well as cross-system and cross-component reports in the SAP NetWeaver BI system, you should consider its implementation in each implementation and extension project in the medium term.

Procurement controlling

On the one hand, reporting is supposed to enable efficient procurement controlling by providing suitable real time reports with an appropriate level of detail. On the other hand, you must meet the requirements of revision-proof documentation of business processes. Procurements without logistic in the Financial Accounting (FI) component have a special position that must be continuously monitored due to their rudimentary, system-based documentation.

Appendices

A   Processes

Based on the objectives of strategic procurement management and the defined roles and tasks in operational purchasing (see Section 3.2, Procurement Organization), the following sections describe the typified target procurement processes for procurement flows in the SAP ERP and SAP SRM landscape.

The target processes 1a to 1c illustrate the work flows for structuring and maintaining the electronic goods catalog in the SAP SRM system, and material master data and outline agreements in the SAP ERP system. The procurement processes 2a and 2b cover the purchasing process for goods and services from the goods catalog und the SAP outline agreements. Individual procurements of goods and services outside the goods catalog and outline agreements with or without participation obligation of the strategic procurement management are outlined in the target processes 3a to 3c. Finally, the presentation of complaints processing and possible escalation rounds out the procurement process work flows. The figures in this chapter illustrate the process flow with all involved roles and tasks. The dot in the figures indicates the starting point of the respective process.

A.1   Process 1a: Structure and Maintenance of the E-Catalog (Push Strategy)

The strategic procurement management, acting as the initiator, determines and centrally negotiates with vendors catalog-capable goods and services based on the classification criteria for goods and services (see Figure 5.40).

After an order has been awarded, the strategic procurement management initiates the migration of data of the selected items, prices, and vendors to the in-house catalog. Catalog management or technical processing can be outsourced by the strategic procurement management to content brokers. However, the strategic procurement management is still responsible for the content.

Data migration to the catalog

157

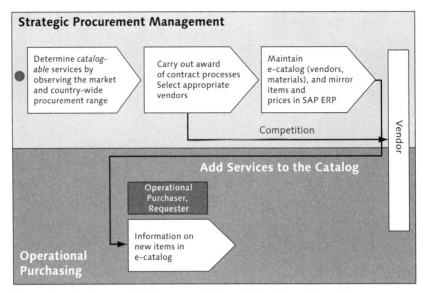

Figure A.1 Structure and Maintenance of the E-Catalog (Push Strategy)

In addition to content management of the goods catalog, end users must be informed proactively by the strategic procurement manager about news and changes in the procurement catalog, for example, new items.

A.2 Process 1b: Structure and Maintenance of Outline Agreements in the SAP System (Push Strategy)

The strategic procurement management centrally creates outline agreements, as well as corresponding master data in the MM component of the SAP ERP system for goods and services that are suitable for outline agreements but not for procurement processing via the SAP SRM system.

Reasons for non-catalogability

Reasons for goods and services to not be suited for inclusion in the catalog could be very low order frequency, few business areas, or a procurement process that is so complex that operational purchasers must implement system-supported procurement in the MM component of the SAP ERP system.

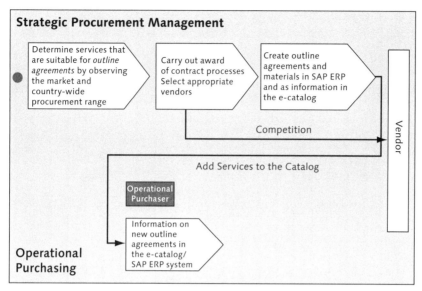

Figure A.2 Structure and Maintenance of Outline Agreements in the SAP System (Push Strategy)

The provisioning of information via the corresponding outline agreements in the SAP ERP system serves to distribute information.

A.3 Process 1c: Structure and Maintenance of the E-Catalog or the Outline Agreements in the SAP System (Pull Strategy)

In contrast to the target processes previously described, the requesters or operational purchasers represent the starting point of the process "Pull Strategy". Requirements of goods and services that have not yet been covered in the goods catalog in the SAP SRM system, or via outline agreements in the SAP ERP system, are forwarded to the strategic procurement management by an operational purchaser.

The SAP SRM system is a suitable medium for entering these requirements. By entering shopping carts with text items, requisitioners can specify their requirement requests. Additionally, technical sketches and descriptions can be added to the text items.

Entry of requirements

159

After the requirements have been grouped and checked against the criteria for the goods and service classification, the strategic procurement manager decides whether further items are added to the goods catalog or whether an outline agreement is created in the SAP ERP system. This decision is influenced in part by the ability of vendors to provide their products in an electronic goods catalog.

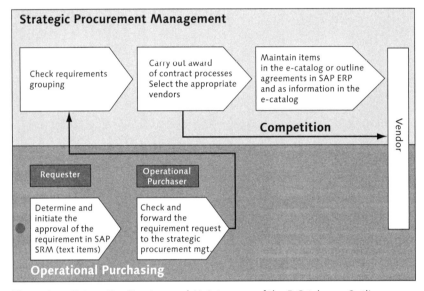

Figure A.3 Retroactive Structure and Maintenance of the E-Catalog or Outline Agreements in the SAP System (Pull Strategy)

A.4 Process 2a: Purchasing of Goods and Services from the E-Catalog

Requisitioners can directly trigger the purchase of goods and services from the electronic goods catalog via the SAP SRM system. Requirement requests defined as shopping carts are automatically forwarded to the approver for each workflow, for release according to existing approval rules. Released shopping carts automatically become purchase orders and are digitally sent to vendors (as XML purchase orders via SAP NetWeaver Exchange Infrastructure [SAP NetWeaver XI]).

When shopping carts are stored, an automatic budget check of the SAP system can be carried out. An automatic account determination and commitment creation also take place in the SAP system for the requested catalog items.

Budget check, account determination, commitment creation

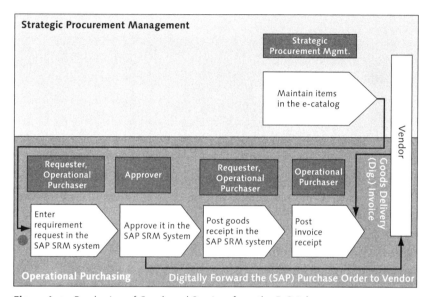

Figure A.4 Purchasing of Goods and Services from the E-Catalog

The goods receipt can be confirmed in the SAP SRM system by both requesters and operational purchasers. Posting of goods receipts through separate goods recipients – for example, warehouse employees – should be approved by a responsible person. The dual-control principle can be adhered to by avoiding that the sender of the purchase order and the person responsible for checking and confirming the goods receipt are the same person.

Confirmation of goods receipt

Invoice entry is automated through electronic data exchange between the vendor and the procuring enterprise. Here, confirmed goods receipts can be settled automatically based on fixed purchase prices (*automatic evaluated receipt settlement* or *self-billing procedure*), or the vendor can receive invoice data via XML data exchange. Ideally, the persons responsible for invoice verification should only become active in case of differences and exceptions.

Electronic data exchange

A.5 Process 2b: Purchasing of Goods and Services from Outside the E-Catalog with MM Outline Agreement

The procurement of goods and services outside the SAP SRM system is generally the responsibility of operational purchasers and can't be implemented by consumers. This means that after they have been entered by the consumer and released by the approver, shopping carts containing items with user-defined text for items that are not included in the catalog are automatically forwarded to the responsible purchaser as a purchase requisition in the SAP system.

Contract release orders

Purchase requisitions are converted into contract release orders with regard to the corresponding outline agreements, and the procurement processing is carried out in the MM component in the SAP ERP system.

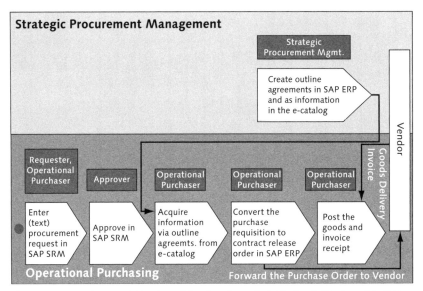

Figure A.5 Purchasing of Goods and Services from Outside the E-Catalog with MM Outline Agreement

In this scenario, the SAP SRM system acts as an information distributor that provides information via the corresponding SAP ERP system outline agreements.

A.6 Process 3a: Individual Procurement of Goods and Services Outside the E-Catalog and Outside the Outline Agreements in MM (Without Participation Obligation)

Individual procurements of goods and services outside the e-catalog are generally implemented in the MM component of the SAP ERP system. The procurement of inventory-managed items is processed primarily via the SAP ERP system because the effort of redundant data retention of these items in the goods catalog and in the SAP ERP system is avoided (see Section 5.2.2, Using Catalog Data).

Individual procurements outside the goods catalog are entered using shopping carts containing items with user-defined text in the SAP SRM system. After a general release by the approver, they are automatically forwarded to the responsible operational purchaser as a purchase requisition in the SAP ERP system. If no participation obligation exists for the strategic procurement management (see Section 3.2.1, Strategic Procurement Management), the purchase requisitions are processed by the purchaser who is responsible from an objective standpoint for the respective material group with system support and full logistical processing via the MM component in the SAP ERP system.

Shopping carts containing items with user-defined text

With regard to the required separation of functions between purchasing, goods receipt, and goods issue, you must balance the high potential of fraudulent actions (with criminal intent) for carrying out central procurement tasks, such as entry of purchase orders and posting of goods issue by one person, against the potentially high logistics costs of personnel separation of individual tasks. In either case, you must establish an effective internal control system, including strict procurement controlling.

Separation of functions between purchasing, goods receipt, and goods issue

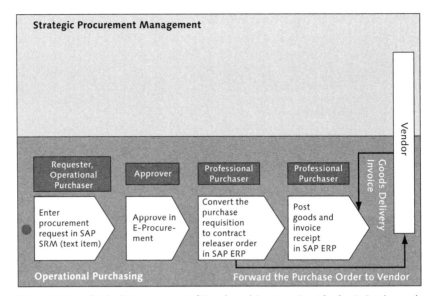

Figure A.6 Individual Procurement of Goods and Services Outside the E-Catalog and Outside the Outline Agreements (Without Participation Obligation of the Strategic Procurement Management) in MM

A.7 Process 3b: Individual Procurement of Goods and Services Outside the E-Catalog and Outside of Outline Agreements in Financial Accounting (FI) (Without Participation Obligation)

In exceptional cases, unpredictable individual procurements can be implemented in the Financial Accounting (FI) component of the SAP ERP system by entering vendor invoices without logistical documentation (see Section 4.2.3 on Consequences for Procurements Without Logistics in Financial Accounting [FI]. Procurements without logistics may be implemented in the following cases:

▸ The goods and services to be procured are not available in the e-catalog, in SAP outline agreements, or as material master data.

▸ No participation obligation exists for the strategic procurement management.

▸ The procurements are authorized exceptions that are in line with compliance guidelines.

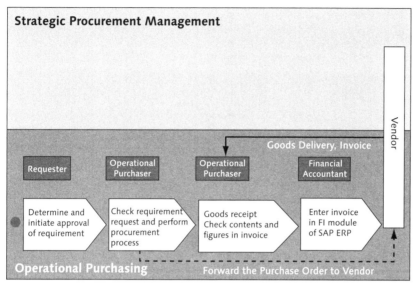

Figure A.7 Individual Procurement of Goods and Services Outside the E-Catalog and Outside of Outline Agreements in Financial Accounting (FI) (Without Participation Obligation of the Strategic Procurement Management)

For these procurement transactions – which are entered in the Financial Accounting (FI) component of the SAP system based on values – the separation of procurement activities and entry of invoices in the SAP system by a financial accountant must be ensured to guarantee the dual-control principle.

Dual-control principle

A.8 Process 3c: Individual Procurement of Goods and Services Outside of the E-Catalog and Outside of Outline Agreements (With Participation Obligation)

For individual procurements of goods and services outside of the e-catalog and outside of outline agreements, with a participation obligation for the strategic procurement management, orders must be placed by the strategic purchasers responsible from a technical standpoint.

As with process 3a, the operational purchasing processing is carried out in the MM component. This clearly indicates that the operational purchaser is the most critical interface to the strategic procurement manager and cooperates with him to place orders.

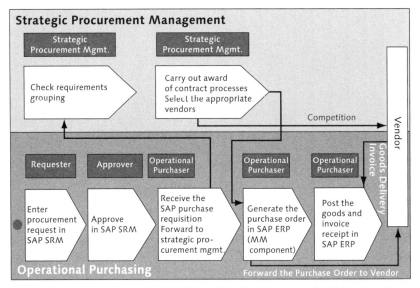

Figure A.8 Individual Procurement of Goods and Services Outside of the E-Catalog and Outside of Outline Agreements (With Participation Obligation of the Strategic Procurement Management)

A.9 Process 4: Processing of Complaints and Escalations

The operational purchaser is the central point of contact in the enterprise for complaints. For procurements from the e-catalog or SAP outline agreements, complaints – for example, regarding quality defects or incorrect goods delivery – are directly forwarded to the vendors by the responsible purchaser.

The strategic procurement management should only be involved in the case of escalation, for example, in the case of failed enforcement of claims.

166

In the context of strategic controlling and vendor management, you can use the vendor evaluation functions in the SAP NetWeaver BI system to enter problems and quality defects that are determined using questionnaires during the entry of goods and invoice receipt in the SAP SRM and SAP ERP systems, and thus include them in the vendor evaluation.

Vendor evaluation

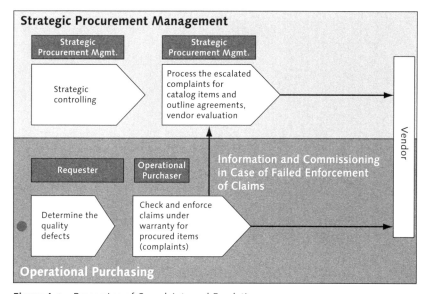

Figure A.9 Processing of Complaints and Escalation

B   Transactions

B.1   Scope of Functions in the Accounts Payable Ledger in the SAP ERP System

The following sections list the standard key transactions of the SAP ERP system, grouped according to business-relevant objects, such as vendor invoice, purchase order, or goods receipt. This provides you with an overview of the scope of functions of the SAP ERP system and the level of support of the individual business-relevant objects.

B.1.1   Invoice Processing for Vendors

Parked Vendor Document (3.1)

- F-63 (Park Vendor Invoice (3.0F))
- F-66 (Park Vendor Credit Memo (3.0F))
- FV60 (Park Incoming Invoices (4.6))
- FV65 (Park Incoming Invoices (4.6))

Vendor Credit Memo (4.6)

- F-41 (Enter Vendor Credit Memo (3.0F))
- FB65 (Enter Incoming Credit Memos (4.6))

Vendor Invoice (4.6)

- F-43 (Enter Vendor Invoice (3.0F))
- FB60 (Enter Incoming Invoices (4.6))

Vendor Open Items (3.1)

- F.41 (A/P: Open Items (3.0F))
- FBL1 (Display Vendor Line Items (3.0F))
- FBL1N (Vendor Line Items (4.6))

- FBL2 (Change Vendor Line Items (3.0F))
- FBL2N (Vendor Line Items (4.6))

Interest Calculation of Open Items (3.1)

- F.4A (Calculation Vendor Interest on Arrears: Post (without OI) (3.0F))
- F.4B (Calculation Vendor Interest on Arrears: Post (with OI) (3.0F))
- F.4C (Calculation Vendor Interest on Arrears: without postings (3.0F))
- F.44 (A/P: Balance Interest Calculation (3.0F))
- F.47 (Vendors: Calculation of Interest on Arrears (3.0F))

Vendor Recurring Entry (3.1)

- FBD5 (Realize Recurring Entry (3.0F))

B.1.2   Special G/L Transactions

Down Payment Request Vendors (3.1)

- F-47 (Down Payment Request (3.0F))
- FBA6 (Vendor Down Payment Request (3.0F))

Down Payment Clearing Vendors (3.1)

- F-54 (Clear Vendor Down Payment (3.0F))
- FBA8 (Clear Vendor Down Payment (3.0F))

Down Payment Made (3.1)

- F-48 (Post Vendor Down Payment (3.0F))
- FBA7 (Post Vendor Down Payment (3.0F))
- /SAPPCE/DPCK01 (Credit-Side Down Payment Chains (4.7))
- /SAPPCE/DPC_LIST_C (Credit-Side Down Payment Chains – List (4.7))

Bill of Exchange Payment (3.1)

▶ F-40 (Bill of Exchange Payment (3.0F))

▶ FBW6 (Vendor Check/Bill of Exchange (3.0F))

▶ FBWD (Returned Bills of Exchange Payable (3.0F))

Payment Request (4.5)

▶ FBP1 (Enter Payment Request (3.0F))

▶ F-59 (Payment Request (3.0F))

B.1.3   Reports (FI – Accounts Payable Accounting)

Analyses Check Processing (4.5)

▶ S_P99_41000101 (Check Register (4.6))

▶ S_P99_41000102 (Check lots (4.6))

▶ S_ALR_87012118 (Bill of Exchange & Check Usage List (4.6))

▶ S_ALR_87012119 (Cashed Checks (4.6))

▶ S_ALR_87012348 (Cashed Checks per Bank Account (4.6))

▶ S_ALR_87012349 (Outstanding Checks Analysis per G/L Account and Vendor (4.6))

▶ FF.4 (Vendor Cashed Checks (3.0F))

▶ FF_4 (Vendor Cashed Checks (4.5B))

▶ S_ALR_87009886 (Cashed Checks per Bank Account (4.6))

▶ S_ALR_87009887 (Outstanding Checks Analysis per G/L Account and Vendor (4.6))

▶ S_ALR_87010068 (Bill of Exchange & Check Usage List (4.6))

▶ S_ALR_87010069 (Cashed Checks (4.6))

Analyses Bill of Exchange Processing (3.1)

▶ S_ALR_87012324 (Extended Bill of Exchange Information (4.6))

▶ S_ALR_87012114 (Bill of Exchange List (4.6))

▸ S_ALR_87012115 (Extended Bill of Exchange List with ABAP
List Viewer (4.6))

Notifications Withholding Tax (3.1)

▸ S_ALR_87012123 (Withholdings and Perceptions – RG 4110 (4.6))

▸ S_ALR_87012125 (Social security withholding (4.6))

▸ S_ALR_87012126 (Data Medium Exchange with Disk (4.6))

▸ S_ALR_87012127 (Payments with Withholding Tax – Argentina
(4.6))

▸ S_ALR_87012128 (Withholding Tax Certificates (4.6))

▸ S_ALR_87012130 (Belgian Withholding Tax Reports 281.50 and
325.50 (4.6))

▸ S_ALR_87012131 (Withholding Tax Report to the Tax Authorities
(Germany) (4.6))

▸ S_ALR_87012133 (Form.770 Withholding Tax Report
Form 770 (4.6))

▸ S_ALR_87012134 (Withholding Tax Report to Vendor (4.6))

▸ S_ALR_87012135 (Withholding Tax Report to the Tax Authorities
(Japan) (4.6))

▸ S_ALR_87012137 (Refundable Withholding Tax (4.6))

▸ S_ALR_87012138 (Withholding Tax Certificates (South Korea) (4.6))

▸ S_ALR_87012139 (Withholding Tax on Business Income
(South Korea) (4.6))

▸ S_ALR_87012140 (Withholding Tax Report (DME) to the Tax Authorities (Spain) (4.6))

▸ S_ALR_87012141 ((Withholding Tax Reporting Model 210 Spain
(4.6))

▸ S_ALR_87010072 (Withholding Tax Report for the Vendor (4.6))

▸ S_ALR_87010073 (Withholdings and Perceptions - RG 4110 (4.6))

▸ S_ALR_87010075 (Social security withholding (4.6))

▸ S_ALR_87010077 (Payments with Withholding Tax – Argentina
(4.6))

▶ S_ALR_87010078 (Withholding Tax Certificates (4.6))

▶ S_ALR_87010080 (Belgian Withholding Tax Reports 281.50 & 325.50 (4.6))

▶ S_ALR_87010081 (Withholding Tax Report to the Tax Authorities (Germany) (4.6))

▶ S_ALR_87010082 (Withholding Tax Report - France (4.6))

▶ S_ALR_87010083 (Form.770 Withholding Tax Report Form 770 (4.6))

▶ S_ALR_87010084 (Withholding Tax Return to Vendor (4.6))

▶ S_ALR_87010085 (Withholding Tax Report to the Tax Authorities (Japan) (4.6))

▶ S_ALR_87010087 (Refundable Withholding Tax (4.6))

▶ S_ALR_87010088 (Withholding Tax Certificates (South Korea) (4.6))

▶ S_ALR_87010089 (Withholding Tax on Business Incomes (South Korea) (4.6))

▶ S_ALR_87010090 (Withholding Tax Report (DME) to the Tax Authorities (Spain) (4.6))

▶ S_ALR_87010091 (Withholding Tax Reporting Model 210 Spain (4.6))

▶ S_ALR_87012122 (Withholding Tax Report for the Vendor (4.6))

Analyses Interest Calculation Processing (3.1)

▶ F.44 (A/P: Balance Interest Calculation (3.0F))

▶ F.47 (Vendors: Calculation of Interest on Arrears (3.0F))

▶ F.48 (Vendors: FI-MM Master Data Comparison (3.0F))

▶ F.4A (Calculation Vendor Interest on Arrears: Post (without OI) (3.0F))

▶ F.4B (Calculation Vendor Interest on Arrears: Post (with OI) (3.0F))

▶ F.4C (Calculation Vendor Interest on Arrears: without postings (3.0F))

▶ S_ALR_87010063 (Vendor Interest Scale (4.6))

▶ S_ALR_87012113 (Vendor Interest Scale (4.6))

Analyses Vendors (3.1)

▸ S_ALR_87012077 (Vendor Information System (4.6))

▸ S_ALR_87012078 (Due Date Analysis for Open Item (4.6))

▸ S_ALR_87012079 (Transaction Figures: Account Balance (4.6))

▸ S_ALR_87012082 (Vendor Balances in Local Currency (4.6))

▸ S_ALR_87012083 (List of Vendor Line Items (4.6))

▸ S_ALR_87012093 (Vendor Business (4.6))

▸ S_ALR_87012103 (List of Vendor Line Items (4.6))

▸ F.40 (Vendor List (3.0F))

▸ S_ALR_87012080 (Transaction Figures: Special Sales (4.6))

▸ S_ALR_87012081 (Transaction Figure: Sales (4.6))

▸ S_ALR_87012084 (Open Items - Vendor Due Date Forecast (4.6))

▸ S_ALR_87012085 (Vendor Appraisal with OI Sorted List (4.6))

▸ S_ALR_87012104 (List of Vendor Line Items (4.6))

▸ S_ALR_87012105 (List of List of Down Payments Open On Key Date – Vendors (4.6C))

B.2   Scope of Functions in Materials Management in the SAP ERP System

B.2.1   Purchase Requisition (3.1)

Regular Transactions

▸ ME51N (Create Purchase Requisition (4.6))

▸ ME52N (Change Purchase Requisition (4.6))

▸ ME53N (Display Purchase Requisition (4.6))

▸ ME53 (Display Purchase Requisition (3.0F))

▸ ME5R (Archived Purchase Requisitions (3.0F))

▸ ME97 (Archive Purchase Requisitions (3.0F))

▸ MEAN (Delivery Addresses (3.0F))

▸ MELB (Purchase Transactions by Tracking No. (3.0F))

- MSRV2 (Service List for Requisition (4.0B))
- ME53N (Display Purchase Requisition (4.6))
- ME5J (Purchase Requisitions for Project (3.1I))
- MECCP_ME2K (For Requisition Account Assignment (4.7))
- ME5W (Resubmission of Purchase Requisitions (3.0F))
- MEMASSRQ (Mass-Changing of Purchase Requisitions (4.6))
- MMPURUIPRCREQ (Create Purchase Order from Purchase Requisition (6.0))

Web Transactions
- MEW6 (Assign Purchase Orders Web (4.0B))
- MEW0 (Procurement Transaction (3.1I))
- MEW1 (Create Requirement Request (3.1I))
- MEW2 (Status Display: Requirement Requests (3.1I))
- MEW3 (Collective Release of Purchase Requests (3.1I))
- MEW4 (Reset Release Purchase Request (3.1I))

Old Transactions
- ME51 (Create Purchase Requisition (3.0F))
- ME52 (Change Purchase Requisition (3.0F))
- ME53 (Display Purchase Requisition (3.0F))

Manual Further Processing
- ME56 (Assign Source to Purchase Requisition (3.0F))
- ME57 (Assign and Process Requisitions (3.0F))
- ME58 (Ordering: Assigned Requisitions (3.0F))

Purchase Requisition Release
- ME54 (Release Purchase Requisition(3.0F))
- ME55 (Collective Release of Purchase Requisition (3.0F))

▸ ME52NB (Buyer Approval: Purchase Requisition (4.7))

▸ ME54N (Release Purchase Requisition (4.7))

▸ MEW3 (Collective Release of Purchase Requests (3.1I))

▸ MEW4 (Reset Release Purchase Request (3.1I))

▸ ME5F (Release Reminder: Purchase Requisition (3.0F))

B.2.2 Purchase Order (3.1)

Regular Transactions

▸ ME21N (Create Purchase Order (4.6))

▸ ME22N (Change Purchase Order (4.6))

▸ MASS_EKKO (PO Mass Maintenance (4.7))

▸ MEMASSRO (Mass Change of Purchase Orders (4.6))

▸ ME25 (Create PO with Source Determination (3.0F))

▸ ME23N (Display Purchase Order (4.6))

▸ ME24 (Maintain Purchase Order Supplement (3.0F))

▸ ME26 (Display PO Supplement (IR) (3.0F))

▸ ME91F (Purchase Orders: Urging/Reminders (4.0B))

▸ ME87 (Aggregate PO History (4.0B))

▸ MEAN (Delivery Addresses (3.0F))

▸ MEPA (Order Price Simulation/Price Info (4.0B))

▸ MEI7 (Change Sales Prices in Purchase Orders (4.5B))

▸ ME59N (Automatic Generation of POs (4.7))

Report Transactions

▸ ME81N (Analysis of Order Values (4.6))

▸ ME81 (Analysis of Order Values (3.0F))

▸ ME1P (Purchase Order Price History (3.0F))

Web Transactions

▸ MEWP (Web based PO (4.5B))

▸ MMPUR_DOCTRK (Document Tracking (EC6-WS))

▸ MEW5 (Collective Release of Purchase Order (3.1I))

▸ MEW9 (mew9 (4.5B))

▸ MEX3 (Display Purchase Document (4.6))

Old Transactions

▸ ME21 (Create Purchase Order (3.0F))

▸ ME22 (Change Purchase Order (3.0F))

▸ ME23 (Display Purchase Order (3.0F))

▸ ME59 (Automatic Generation of POs (3.0F))

Order Optimization

▸ WLB1 (Investment Buying (4.0B))

▸ WLB3 (Automatic Optimization PO-Based Load Building (4.0B))

▸ WLB5 (Manual Load Building (4.0B))

▸ WLB13 (Automatic Load Building (4.6))

▸ WLB2 (Investment Buying Analysis (4.0B))

▸ WLB4 (Results List for Automatic Load Building (4.0B))

▸ WLB6 (Investment Buying Simulation (4.0B))

▸ WLB7 (Analysis for Service Level (4.0B))

▸ WLB8 (Simulation for Quantity Optimizing (4.5B))

▸ WLBA (Configuration Check for Load Building (4.6C))

▸ WLBB (Vendor Service Level (4.6C))

▸ WLBA_CUS (Customizing Analysis for Load Building (4.6))

Release

▸ ME28 (Release Purchase Order (3.0F))

▸ ME29N (Release Purchase Order (4.7))

B.2.3 Request (3.1)

Regular Transactions

▸ ME41 (Create Request For Quotation (3.0F))

▸ ME42 (Change Request For Quotation (3.0F))

▸ ME43 (Display Request For Quotation (3.0F))

▸ ME4B (RFQs by Requirement Tracking Number (3.0F))

▸ ME4C (RFQs by Material Group (3.0F))

▸ ME4L (RFQs by Vendor (3.0F))

▸ ME4M (RFQs by Material (3.0F))

▸ ME4N (RFQs by RFQ Number (3.0F))

▸ ME4S (RFQs by Collective Number (3.0F))

▸ ME80A (Purchasing Reporting: RFQs (4.0B))

▸ ME80AN (General Analyses (A) (4.6))

▸ ME44 (Maintain RFQ Supplement (3.0F))

▸ ME45 (Release RFQ (3.0F))

B.2.4 Offer (3.1)

Regular Transactions

▸ ME47 (Create Quotation (3.0F))

▸ ME91A (Urge Submission of Quotations (4.0B))

▸ ME1E (Quotation Price History (3.0F))

▸ ME49 (Price Comparison List (3.0F))

▸ ME48 (Display Quotation (3.0F))

B.2.5 Contract (3.1)

Regular Transactions

▸ ME31K (Create Contract (4.0B))

▸ ME32K (Change Contract (4.0B))

▸ ME33K (Display Contract (4.0B))

- ME33 (Display Outline Agreement (3.0F))
- ME34K (Maintain Contract Supplement (4.0B))
- ME34 (Maintain Outline Agreement Supplement (3.0F))
- ME36 (Display Agreement Supplement (IR) (3.0F))
- ME31 (Create Outline Agreement (3.0F))
- ME32 (Change Outline Agreement (3.0F))
- ME3P (Recalculate Contract Price (3.0F))
- MEMASSCONTRACT (Mass Changing of Contracts (6.0))

Report Transactions
- ME80R (Purchasing Reporting: Outline Agreements (4.0B))
- ME80RN (General Analyses (L,K) (4.6))
- ME3K (Outline Agreements by Account Assignment (3.0F))
- ME3B (Outline Agreements per Requirement Number (3.0F))
- ME3C (Outline Agreements by Material Group (3.0F))
- ME3J (Outline Agreements per Project (3.1I))
- ME3L (Outline Agreements per Vendor (3.0F))
- ME3M (Outline Agreements by Material (3.0F))
- ME3N (Outline Agreements by Agreement Number (3.0F))

Release
- ME35K (Release Contract (4.0B))
- ME35 (Release Outline Agreement (3.0F))

B.2.6 Acknowledgement (3.1)

Regular Transactions
- ME92 (Monitor Order Acknowledgment (3.0F))
- ME92F (Monitor Order Acknowledgment (4.0B))
- ME92K (Monitor Order Acknowledgment (4.0B))
- ME92L (Monitor Order Acknowledgment (4.0B))

▸ ME2A (Monitor Confirmations (3.0F))

B.2.7 Urging and Reminding

Regular Transactions

▸ ME91 (Purchasing Documents: Urging/Reminding (3.0F))

▸ ME91F (Purchase Orders: Urging/Reminders (4.0B))

▸ ME91E (Scheduling Agreement Schedules: Urging/Remind (4.0B))

B.2.8 Goods Receipt (3.1)

Regular Transactions

▸ MIGO (Goods Movement (4.6))

▸ MIGO_GO (Goods Movement (4.6))

▸ MIGO_GR (Goods Movement (4.6))

▸ MB31 (Goods Receipt for Production Order (3.0F))

▸ MB1C (Other Goods Receipts (3.0F))

▸ MB02 (Change Material Document (3.0F))

▸ MB03 (Display Material Document (3.0F))

▸ MBAD (Delete Material Documents (3.0F))

▸ MBBM (Batch Input: Post Material Document (3.0F))

▸ MESF (Release Blocked Stock via Material Document (3.0F))

▸ MBSL (Copy Material Document (3.0F))

▸ MBSU (Place in Storage for Material Document: Initial Screen (3.0F))

▸ MBNL (Subsequent Delivery for Material Document (4.6))

▸ MBPM (Manage Held Data (4.6))

▸ MB5OA (Display Valuated GR Blocked Stock (6.0))

▸ ME2V (Goods Receipt Forecast (3.0F))

Old Transactions

▸ MB01 (Post Goods Receipt for PO (3.0F))

▸ MB0A (Post Goods Receipt for PO (3.0F))

‣ MB11 (Goods Movement (3.0F))

B.2.9 Transfer Posting/Stock Transfer (3.1)

Regular Transactions

‣ MB5T (Stock in Transit CC (4.0B))

‣ MIGO_TR (Transfer Posting (4.6))

Old Transactions

‣ MB1B (Transfer Posting (3.0F))

B.2.10 Return Delivery (3.1)

Regular Transactions

‣ MBRL (Return Delivery for Material Document (3.0F))

‣ MBGR (Display Material Documents by Movement Reason (3.0F))

B.2.11 External Services Purchasing

Regular Transactions

‣ MSRV4 (Service List for RFQ (4.0B))

‣ MSRV2 (Service List for Requisition (4.0B))

B.2.12 Purchase Order for External service (3.1)

Regular Transactions

‣ MSRV3 (Service List for Purchase Order (4.0B))

‣ ME2S (Services per Purchase Order (4.0B))

B.2.13 Contract for External Services (3.1)

Regular Transactions

‣ ME3S (Service List for Contract (4.0B))

‣ MSRV5 (Service List for Contract (4.0B))

B.2.14 Acceptance of External Services

Regular Transactions

▸ ML81 (Maintain Service Entry Sheet (3.0F))

▸ ML81N (Service Entry Sheet (4.6))

▸ ML82 (Display Service Entry Sheet (3.0F))

▸ ML83 (Message Processing: Service Entry (3.0F))

▸ ML84 (List of Service Entry Sheets (3.0F))

▸ ML86 (Import Service Data (3.0F))

▸ ML92 (Entry Sheets for Service (3.0F))

▸ MN13 (Create Message: Service Entry Sheet (3.0F))

▸ MN14 (Change Message: Service Entry Sheet (3.0F))

▸ MN15 (Display Message: Service Entry Sheet (3.0F))

▸ MEL0 (Service Entry Sheet (3.0F))

▸ ML85 (Collective Release of Entry Sheets (3.0F))

Web Transactions

▸ MEW10 (Service Entry in Web (4.5B))

▸ MEW7 (Release of Service Entry Sheets (4.0B))

▸ MEW8 (Release of Service Entry Sheet (4.0B))

▸ MEWS (Service Entry (Component) (4.5B))

Report Transactions

▸ MSRV1 (List for Service (4.0B))

▸ MSRV2 (Service List for Requisition (4.0B))

▸ MSRV3 (Service List for Purchase Order (4.0B))

▸ MSRV4 (Service List for RFQ (4.0B))

▸ MSRV5 (Service List for Contract (4.0B))

▸ MSRV6 (Service List for Entry Sheet (4.0B))

B.2.15   Invoicing Plan (3.1)

Regular Transactions

- ▶ MLRP (Periodic Invoicing Plans (4.0B))
- ▶ MRIS (Settle Invoicing Plan (4.0B))

B.2.16   Invoice Parking (3.1)

Regular Transactions

- ▶ MIR7 (Park Invoice (4.6))
- ▶ MR41 (Park Invoice (3.0F))
- ▶ MR44 (Post Parked Document (3.0F))
- ▶ MR43 (Display Parked Invoice (3.0F))
- ▶ MR42 (Change Parked Invoice (3.0F))

B.2.17   Evaluated Receipt Settlement

Regular Transactions

- ▶ MRRL (Evaluated Receipt Settlement (4.0B))
- ▶ MRRS (Evaluated Receipt Settlement (3.0F))
- ▶ MRER (Evaluated Receipt Settlement (ERS) Automotive (6.0))
- ▶ MRDC (Automatic Settlement of Planned Delivery Costs (ERS) (6.0))

B.2.18   Vendor Invoice Receipt (3.1)

Regular Transactions

- ▶ MIRO (Enter Invoice (4.6))
- ▶ MR03 (Display Invoice Verification Document (3.0F))
- ▶ MR3M (Display Invoice Document (3.0F))
- ▶ MRED (EDI Invoice Receipt (4.0B))
- ▶ MIR4 (Call MIRO - Change Status (4.6))
- ▶ MR5M (Delete Invoice Document (4.0B))
- ▶ MR00 (Invoice Verification (3.0F))
- ▶ MRMO (Logistics Invoice Verification (3.0F))

▸ MR02 (Process Blocked Invoices (3.0F))

▸ MRBR (Release Blocked Invoices (4.6))

Report Transactions

▸ MIR5 (Display List of Invoice Documents (5.0))

▸ MIR6 (Invoice Overview (4.6))

▸ MR1B (Overview Result of Invoice Verification (4.0B))

▸ MR51 (Material Line Items (3.0F))

▸ MB5U (Analyze Conversion Differences (4.6))

Old Transactions

▸ MR01 (Process Incoming Invoice (3.0F))

▸ MR1M (Process Incoming Invoice (3.0F))

▸ MR2M (Change Invoice Document (4.0B))

▸ MRHR (Enter Invoice (3.0F))

B.2.19 Vendor Credit Memo (3.1)

Regular Transactions

▸ MR8M (Cancel Invoice Document (3.0F))

▸ MR08 (Cancel Invoice Document (3.0F))

▸ MR1G (Enter Incoming Credit Memo (3.0F))

▸ MRHG (Enter Credit Memo (3.0F))

▸ MB5L (List of Stock Values: Balances (3.0F))

B.2.20 Purchasing Rebate (3.1)

Regular Transactions

▸ MEB4 (Settlement re Vendor Rebate Arrangements (3.0F))

▸ MEB0 (Reversal of Settlement Runs (4.6))

▸ MEBE (Workflow Settlement re Vendor Rebate Arrangements (4.0B))

▸ MEU2 (Perform Business Volume Comparison: Rebate (3.0F))

▶ MEBB (Check Open Documents, Vendor Rebate Arrangements (3.0F))

▶ MEBD (Subsequent Vendor Sales with Document Adjustment (4.0B))

▶ MEBF (Updating of External Business Volumes (4.0B))

▶ MEBI (Message, Subsequent Settlement – Settlement Run (4.6))

▶ MEBJ (Recompile Income, Vendor Rebate Arrangements (4.5B))

▶ MEU0 (Assign User to User Group (4.6))

▶ MEU3 (Display Business Volume Comparison: Rebate (3.0F))

▶ WB00 (Subsequent Settlement (3.0F))

▶ MEU5 (Display Business Volume Comparison: Rebate (4.6))

▶ MEU4 (Display Business Volume Comparison: Rebate (4.6))

▶ MEIA (New Structure Document Index Customer Settlement (4.7))

Report Transactions

▶ MEBA (Comp. Suppl. BV, Vendor Rebate Arrangement (3.0F))

▶ MEBM (List of Settlement Runs for Arrangements (4.5B))

▶ MEBS (Statement Settlement Documents, Vendor Rebate Arrangements (4.5B))

B.2.21 Physical Inventory Document (3.1)

▶ MI01 (Create Physical Inventory Document (3.0F))

▶ MI02 (Change Physical Inventory Document (3.0F))

▶ MI12 (Display Changes (4.5B))

▶ MI24 (Physical Inventory List (4.5B))

▶ MIMD (Transfer PDC Physical Inventory Data (3.0F))

▶ MI22 (Display Physical Inventory Documents for Material (3.0F))

▶ MI23 (Display Physical Inventory Data for Material (3.0F))

▶ MI9A (Analyze Archived Physical Inventory Documents (3.0F))

▶ MIAD (Delete Physical Inventory Documents (3.0F))

▶ MIAL (Inventory Documents: Read Archive (3.0F))

▶ MIDO (Physical Inventory Overview (3.0F))

▶ MI21 (Print Physical Inventory Document (3.0F))

▶ MI03 (Display Physical Inventory Document (3.0F))

▶ MI00 (Physical Inventory (3.0F))

B.2.22 Inventory Difference (3.1)

▶ MI08 (Create List of Differences with Document (3.0F))

▶ MI10 (Create List of Differences without Document (3.0F))

▶ MI07 (Process List of Differences (3.0F))

▶ MI20 (Print List of Differences (3.0F))

▶ MI11 (Recount Physical Inventory Document (3.0F))

B.2.23 Cycle Counting Document (3.1)

▶ MIBC (ABC Analysis for Cycle Counting (3.0F))

▶ MICN (Batch Input: Physical Inventory Documents for Cycle Counting (3.0F))

B.2.24 Sample-Based Physical Inventory Document (3.1)

▶ MBSI (Find Inventory Sampling (3.0F))

▶ MIS1 (Create Inventory Sampling – ERP (3.0F))

▶ MIS2 (Change Inventory Sampling (3.0F))

▶ MIS5 (Create Inventory Sampling - Other (3.0F))

▶ MIS3 (Display Inventory Sampling (3.0F))

▶ MIS4 (Create Inventory Sampling - R/2 (3.0F))

B.2.25 Price Change (3.1)

▶ MR21 (Price Change (3.0F))

▶ CKMPCSEARCH (Price Change Documents for Material (4.5B))

▶ S_P99_41000062 (Material List: Prices and Inventory Values (4.6))

▶ CKMPRP (Maintain Planned Prices (4.0B))

▸ CKMPRP2 (Maintain Future Prices by Profile (4.5B))

▸ CKMPRPN (Price Maintenance (4.6))

▸ CKMTOPPRICEDIF (Material with Highest Difference in V Price (4.6))

▸ CKMTOPSTOCKVAL (Materials with Highest Inventory Value (4.6))

▸ MR2B (Activate Future Prices (3.0F))

▸ CKME (Activation of Planned Prices (4.0B))

B.2.26 Material Debit/Credit (3.1)

▸ MR22 (Material Debit/Credit (3.0F))

▸ CKMLDC (Debit/Credit Material (4.5B))

B.2.27 Stock Value Adjustment (3.1)

▸ MRN9 (Balance Sheet Values by Account (3.0F))

B.2.28 Determination of Lowest Value (3.1)

▸ MRN3 (Loss-Free Valuation (4.5B))

▸ MRN0 (Determination of Lowest Value: Market Prices (3.0F))

▸ MRN1 (Determination of Lowest Value: Range of Coverage (3.0F))

▸ MRN2 (Determination of Lowest Value: Movement Rate (3.0F))

▸ MRN8 (Lowest Value: Price Variances (3.0F))

▸ MRN1_TS (Determine Lowest Value: Range of Coverage (4.6))

▸ MRN1_RB (Determine Lowest Value: Range of Coverage (4.6))

▸ MRNB (Revaluation (4.5B))

▸ MRLD (Transfer Valuation Prices (4.0B))

▸ CKU1 (Update Material Price (3.0F))

B.2.29 LIFO Valuation (3.1)

▸ MRL9 (LIFO Valuation: Create Document Extract (3.0F))

▸ MRL6 (Select Materials (3.0F))

- MRLK (LIFO: Adjust Units of Measure (4.5B))
- MRLF (Create Version as Copy (4.0B))
- MR32 (Change Material Layer (LIFO) (3.0F))
- MRLI (Generate Pools (4.0B))
- MRL7 (Display Pool Formation (3.0F))
- MRLE (Change Group Structure (4.0B))
- MRLJ (LIFO Data Transfer (4.5B))
- MRLH (Change LIFO/FIFO Valuation Level (4.0B))
- MR39 (Display Documents (LIFO) (3.0F))
- MRL1 (Perform LIFO Valuation: Single Material (3.0F))
- MRL4 (Display LIFO Valuation: Single Material (3.0F))
- MRL3 (LIFO Lowest Value Comparison (3.0F))

B.2.30 FIFO Valuation (3.1)

- MRF4 (FIFO: Select Materials (3.0F))
- MRF3 (FIFO Valuation: Create Document Extract (3.0F))
- MRF1 (Execute FIFO Valuation (3.0F))
- MR34 (Change FIFO Data (3.0F))
- MR35 (Display FIFO Data (3.0F))
- MRF2 (Display Documents (FIFO) (3.0F))
- MRF5 (FIFO: Delete Valuation Data (3.0F))

B.2.31 Material Ledger (3.1)

- MRY4 (Transfer ML Prices (4.7))
- S_ALR_87013180 (Listing of Materials by Period Status (4.6))
- S_ALR_87013181 (Material Ledger Data Over Several Periods (4.6))
- S_ALR_87013182 (Transaction History for a Material (4.6))
- CKMB (Display Material Ledger Document (4.0B))
- CKMS (Material Ledger Documents for Material (4.0B))

▶ CKMSTART (Production Startup of Material Ledger (4.0B))

▶ CKMLCPMLBF (Material Ledger Budget Cockpit (4.7))

▶ CKM3VERYOLD (Display Material Ledger Data (4.7))

B.2.32 Vendor Consignment Stock (3.1)

▶ MSK3 (Display Vendor Consignment Goods (3.0F))

▶ MB54 (Consignment Stocks (3.0F))

▶ MSK1 (Create Vendor Consignment Goods (3.0F))

▶ MSK2 (Change Vendor Consignment Goods (3.0F))

▶ MSK5 (Vendor Consignment: Activate Future Price (3.0F))

▶ MRKO (Consignment and Pipeline Settlement (3.0F))

▶ MSK4 (Display Vendor Consignment Changes (3.0F))

B.2.33 Stock of Material Provided Subcontracting (3.1)

▶ ME2O (SC Stock Monitoring (Vendor) (3.0F))

▶ MBLB (Stocks at Subcontractor (4.6))

▶ MB04 (Subsequent Adjustment of "Material Provided" Consumption (3.0F))

▶ MIGO_GS (Subsequent Adjustment of Material Provided (4.7))

B.2.34 Customer Consignment Stock/ Returnable Packaging Stock (3.1)

▶ MB58 (Consignment and Return Packaging at Customer (3.0F))

▶ MMG1 (Create Returnable Packaging & (4.6))

▶ MRKO (Consignment and Pipeline Settlement (3.0F))

B.2.35 Overviews Stocks (3.1)

▶ MB51 (Material Document List (3.0F))

▶ MB52 (List of Warehouse Stocks on Hand (3.0F))

▶ MB53 (Display Plant Stock Availability (3.0F))

▸ MB59 (Material Document List (3.0F))

▸ MMBE (Stock Overview (3.0F))

▸ CO09 (Availability Overview (3.0F))

▸ ENGR (Periodic Declarations (4.6C))

B.2.36 Aggregations Material Valuation (3.1)

▸ MB5L (List of Stock Values: Balances (3.0F))

▸ MB5S (Display List of GR/IR Balances (3.0F))

▸ MB5W (List of Stock Values (3.0F))

▸ MB5K (Stock Consistency Check (4.5B))

▸ MB5B (Stocks for Posting Date (3.0F))

B.2.37 Aggregations Batch Management (3.1)

▸ MB56 (Analyze Batch Where-Used List (3.0F))

▸ MB57 (Compile Batch Where-Used List (3.0F))

▸ MB5C (Pick-Up List (3.0F))

▸ MB5M (BBD/Production Date (3.0F))

▸ MB5E (Create Batch Where-Used Archive (3.0F))

▸ MB5D (Delete Documents of Batch Where-Used File (3.0F))

▸ MB5A (Evaluate Batch Where-Used Archive (3.0F))

B.2.38 Aggregations Inventory (3.1)

▸ MIDO (Physical Inventory Overview (3.0F))

▸ MI22 (Display Physical Inventory Documents for Material (3.0F))

▸ MI23 (Display Physical Inventory Data for Material (3.0F))

▸ MI24 (Physical Inventory List (4.5B))

C   List of Abbreviations

AG	Aktiengesellschaft (German stock corporation)
PReq	Purchase requisition
BI	Business Intelligence
BW	Business Information Warehouse
CO	Controlling
DCGK	German Corporate Governance Codex
DP	Data processing
EDI	Electronic Data Interchange
ERP	Enterprise Resource Planning
FI	Financial Accounting
GAAP	Generally Accepted Accounting Principles
CG	Corporate Governance
GCC	German Commercial Code
IT	Information Technology
MM	Materials Management
RBE	Reverse Business Engineering
SRM	Supplier Relationship Management
SOX	Sarbanes-Oxley Act

D   Authors

Dr. Eduard Gerhardt is project manager at IBIS Prof. Thome AG. He was responsible for the scientific support of the procurement organization's reorganization and the implementation of SAP SRM within the SAP implementation project at the Hessian state government in Germany. In addition, he is responsible for developing implementation and analysis tools for SAP software in the areas of financial accounting, funds management, and materials management. He is also a lecturer at the University of Würzburg.

Kai Krüger is an instructor at the Hessian ministry of finance. He is responsible for the development of the project "Implementation of the new administration control with SAP in the Hessian state government" and of business-relevant concepts and their implementation using SAP. His field of expertise includes accounting and finance, as well as controlling and development of reporting systems.

Dr. Oliver Schipp is a project manager at IBIS Prof. Thome AG. He provides controlling and scientific support for the SAP implementation project at the Hessian state government He has implemented the Controlling (CO) component of Accounting and SAP Business Warehouse (BW) in various SAP projects and is responsible for the development of implementation and analysis tools for the Controlling (CO) component of Accounting. He is also a lecturer at the University of Würzburg.

Index

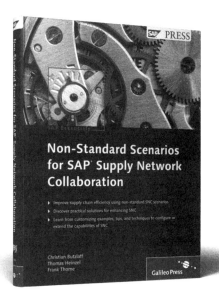

Teaches how to integrate cProjects and
RPM to provide a high-level visibility
over the entire project portfolio

Provides functionality and integration
details for cProjects and RPM with
SAP Project System

Includes real-world customer
examples throughout

Up-to-date for cProjects 4.5 and RPM 4.5

approx. 320 pp., 68,– Euro / US$ 85
ISBN 978-1-59229-224-0, Nov 2008

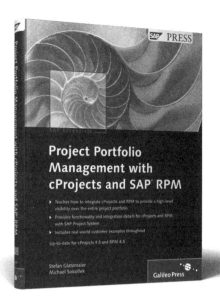

Project Portfolio Management with cProjects and SAP RPM

www.sap-press.com

Stefan Glatzmaier, Michael Sokollek

Project Portfolio Management with cProjects and SAP RPM

SAP PRESS Essentials 49

This essentials guide introduces and teaches users
how to integrate and use project portfolio management with SAP to support their business processes.
The book focuses on cProjects and SAP RPM, as well
as the integration with SAP Project System. With
real-life examples, this book uses examples to illustrate specific solution options and projects. The main
chapters are based on the actual business processes
in an enterprise and contain industry-specific recom-
mendations. The book is based on the latest releases,
and is a must-have addition to any SAP library.

>> www.sap-press.de/1838

Introduces readers to the
ins-and-outs of SAP DMS

Addresses all uses and details of
Document Management

Provides real-world
examples and practical

Up-to-date for ERP 6.0

approx. 130 pp., 68,– Euro / US$ 85
ISBN 978-1-59229-240-0, Jan 2009

Effective Document
Management with SAP DMS

www.sap-press.com

Eric Stajda

Effective Document Management
with SAP DMS

This essentials guide is a complete and practical
resource to SAP Document Management System. It teaches project managers, functional
users, and consultants everything they need to
know to understand, configure, and use SAP
DMS, and provides step-by-step instructions
and real-world scenarios. This is a must-have
book for anyone interested in learning about
and creating an efficient, effective document
management system using SAP.

>> www.sap-press.de/1936

Learn how to integrate SAP SRM with other core SAP components

Uncover key insights on strategies, functionalities, and methodologies

695 pp., 2007, 69,95 Euro / US$ 69,95
ISBN 978-1-59229-068-0

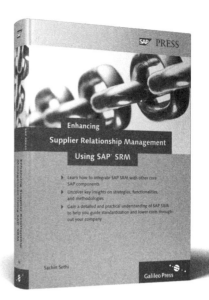

Enhancing Supplier Relationship Management Using SAP SRM

www.sap-press.com

Sachin Sethi

Enhancing Supplier Relationship Management Using SAP SRM

This book will help readers leverage valuable insights into strategies and methodologies for implementing SAP SRM to enhance procurement in their companies.
Tips and tricks, changes brought about by 5.0 and customization will be woven in throughout the book. It will provide detailed information on integration and dependencies of mySAP SRM with core SAP components like MM, IM, FI and HR.

ISBN 978-1-59229-209-7

© 2009 by Galileo Press Inc., Boston (MA)
1st Edition 2009

German Edition first published 2008 by Galileo Press, Bonn, Germany.

Galileo Press is named after the Italian physicist, mathematician and philosopher Galileo Galilei (1564–1642). He is known as one of the founders of modern science and an advocate of our contemporary, heliocentric worldview. His words *Eppur si muove* (And yet it moves) have become legendary. The Galileo Press logo depicts Jupiter orbited by the four Galilean moons, which were discovered by Galileo in 1610.

Editor   Eva Tripp
English Edition Editor   Meg Dunkerley
Translation   Lemoine International, Inc., Salt Lake City, UT
Copy Editor   Jutta VanStean
Cover Design   Silke Braun
Photo Credit   Masterfile/Damir Frkovic
Layout Design   Vera Brauner
Production   Iris Warkus
Typesetting   Publishers' Design and Production Services, Inc.
Printed and bound in Canada

Interested in reading more?

Please visit our Web site for all
new book releases from SAP PRESS.

www.sap-press.com